The Home Equity Survival Guide

The Home Equity Survival Guide

Michael Moebs Kenneth Williams
Eva Moebs

Longman Financial Services Publishing
a division of Longman Financial Services Institute, Inc.

While a great deal of care has been taken to provide accurate and current information, the ideas, suggestions, general principles and conclusions presented in this book are subject to local, state and federal laws and regulations, court cases and any revisions of same. The reader is thus urged to consult legal counsel regarding any points of law — this publication should not be used as a substitute for competent legal advice.

Executive Editor: Kathleen A. Welton
Project Editor: Roseann P. Costello
Copy Editor: Richard Weisenseel
Interior Design: Edwin Harris
Cover Design: Robert Cooley

Published by Longman Financial Services Publishing
a division of Longman Financial Services Intstitute, Inc.

Printed in the United States of America.

88 89 90 10 9 8 7 6 5 4 3 2 1

Library of Congress Cataloging-in-Publication Data

Moebs, Michael.
The home equity survival guide/Michael Moebs, Eva Moebs, Kenneth Williams.
p. cm.
Includes index.
ISBN 0-88462-735-7
1. Home equity loans United States Handbooks, manuals, etc.
I. Moebs, Eva. II. Williams, Kenneth, 1946 . III. Title.
HG2040.45.M64 1988
332.7'22'0973 dc19 88 10108

Contents

Illustrations

Illustrations

Table

Chapter One

Introduction

Mike Moebs and Ken Williams have just concluded a successful business arrangement. They decide to stop at a local watering hole to celebrate before catching the train home. These guys really know how to set the right priorities.

"This looks like the same old place," says Ken. "It hasn't changed a bit."

As they pull up stools to the bar, Joe, the bartender, comes over. "Ken! I haven't seen you in a long time!"

"It's nice to see you, Joe!"

"What's been keeping you out of City Tavern?"

"Well, I no longer work downtown for Citicorp Savings, Joe. I joined Mike here in his company."

"Mike, I haven't seen you for a while either! So, what'll you have?"

"Two cold ones. We're celebrating a successful meeting."

Joe says, "What are you guys up to?"

"Well," says Mike, "My firm, which does research in training, software, and publications, just finished a new book called The Home Equity Survival Guide."

"You mean how to get a home equity loan?"

"That's right, Joe."

"Well, isn't that a coincidence. Sitting right next to you, around the bend of the bar, is Floyd. Floyd, come on over here. I'd like you to meet Ken Williams and Mike Moebs. These guys are the experts in financial services and home equity loans you've been looking for."

After a round of introductions, Joe pops a question.

"Ken and Mike, Floyd here has been telling me he's interested in getting a home equity loan but he doesn't know anything about them."

Floyd says, "Yeah, that's right. What do you guys know about home equity loans? I'm interested in getting one. My accountant tells me I should get one, and my wife keeps pushing me that we should add an addition to our house 'cause our family is growing, and it just seems to me that if I'm going to do all these things I better go out and get a home equity loan. It's either that or get a new accountant and a new wife, but it's hard to find a good accountant these days!"

Mike pops in. "Being a CPA, I can sympathize with that! But seriously, do you itemize your income taxes?"

"Yes I do, as a matter of fact. Why, does that matter?"

"It sure does, Floyd, because the Tax Reform Act of 1986 says interest on personal loans will be phased out over a period of four years."

"Well, you know," says Floyd, "I've got two car loans plus credit cards charges from Christmas and some old student loans that we're paying off. And of course I've got the home mortgage. When you stop to think about it, I have my fair share of debt."

"Most people do, Floyd," says Ken. "And that's why it's so important that you try to economize every way you can, because you do have those bills and loans to pay off. Why not let the new tax law help you do that."

"Well, how much should I get in a home equity loan?"

"It's less a matter of how much you should get, Floyd, and more of what you're going to borrow for. You should always have a good reason to borrow. Now, take your two car loans and credit cards. Do you know how much interest you're paying?"

"Yes, it's at least $100 a month."

"Well, that's $1,200 a year," says Ken, "and you're used to deducting all of that on your taxes. But you're going to be losing that whole deduction. So there's a good reason right there to borrow under a home equity loan. Also, Floyd, you mentioned that you wanted to add an addition to your home. That's another good reason, since you're borrowing at the same time as you're adding additional equity."

"That certainly makes sense. I just wonder, though—are there any bad reasons for getting a home equity loan?"

"There sure are. In fact, there are some reasons that are dangerous enough to be potentially hazardous to your well-being, especially if you choose the wrong type of home equity loan."

"Boy, I'd better be careful!" says Floyd. "I didn't realize there were different types of home equity loans."

"Sure, there are at least two," says Mike, "the line of credit and the fixed rate closed end loan or the regular term loan that looks like a car loan."

"Well, what else should I look for when getting a home equity loan?"

Ken says, "First ask yourself if you can afford the payments. There is a rule of thumb that you can follow to help you—it's called the debt ratio."

"You know, that's a good benchmark. Right now, I'm only at about 25 percent or 30 percent of gross income right now."

"Then you might be able to get a home equity loan."

"Before you decide to go shopping around, though," says Mike, "you need to ask yourself whether you can stand two mortgages."

"What do you mean?"

"Well, you probably have a first mortgage on the house, and now you are going to get a second mortgage to pay for home improvement and consolidate bills so that you can deduct interest. You're looking at a long-term commitment. So ask yourself, can you stand two monthly payments for ten or fifteen years?"

"I probably can. But then again, I don't know if my wife can."

Mike adds his two cents. "Yeah, Floyd, that's important 'cause that's a psychological aspect of borrowing, and you should definitely take that into consideration."

"Assuming I can stand the extra debt, you guys keep mentioning the tax issues. Another question I have is on those tax aspects. I don't really quite understand how that all works."

"This is getting pretty complicated, Floyd," says Mike. "We could be here awhile with all this advice."

"Well, what if I buy you guys another beer?"

"I've got a better idea—why don't you buy our book? We just happen to have a copy of it right here with us."

"Oh, let me see it—*The Home Equity Survival Guide*. Boy, this looks interesting. I should have this."

Mike says, "Just give us the cash, and we'll be happy to let you have it, Floyd."

"How about a check?"

"Sure," says Ken, "if you have two pieces of identification and if Joe here will co-sign for it."

"Floyd," says Joe, "watch out for these guys. Remember, they were both lenders and they never lost a penny!"

Everyone laughs. Ken and Mike say that they have to catch the 5:27 and take their leave after wishing the best to Floyd in his search for a home equity loan.

While this is a fictitious situation, it is close to the many encounters that Mike Moebs and Ken Williams run into on a day-to-day basis in their travels while doing training seminars for lenders. It also highlights how a lot of people do their financial planning and the "procedures" that they follow when trying to obtain a loan.

This book presents a more systematic approach. If you decide that you want a home equity loan, it will guide you through the maze of programs, products and features that you'll encounter and then help you get the best deal. It will tell you what to look for among the documents you will see and what you can expect at the closing. And it will advise you about what to do if you get into trouble with making the payments. Most important, it will help you decide whether or not you really need a home equity loan and what type of home equity loan you should get.

Why Do You Need This Book?

An article in the Chicago Tribune read as follows*:

"The suburban Westchester retiree finally gave up trying to get her tax question answered by calling the IRS hot line.

"'It's terrible over the phone,' she said... 'They couldn't answer any of my questions. I've gotten cut off a number of times....it's very aggravating.'

"...there's an added level of confusion and frustration as the nation wades through the first year of tax reform. Professional tax preparers and the IRS often are as confused as taxpayers.

"That fact hit home last week, when the General Accounting Office, the investigative arm of Congress, reported that 39 percent of

---

* "Tax reform confusing—even to IRS," *Chicago Tribune*, 28 February 1988.

questions put to the IRS' toll-free help numbers were answered incorrectly.
"The IRS said the number was 25 percent, but agreed it was hardly a stellar showing."*

So the first answer to the question of why you need this book is that you'd better understand something about the new tax issues, because not even the government can answer your questions correctly.

And second, there are about 57 million homeowners in the U.S., which is about 65 percent of the population. It's estimated that there is about $1 trillion of equity in those homes. Based on research from various sources, there are probably 830,000 homeowners who have a home equity loan right now. Now, the estimated number of people who have problems paying off their loans is almost two percent of those, or over 15,000 households.* These people, like yourself, looked at a home equity loan and decided to get one but couldn't handle it and ended up in trouble.

You could be in that two percent. This is another very good reason why you need to understand something about this subject.

A home equity loan is like the story of the lady and the tiger. Behind one door is a beautiful woman and behind the other one is a tiger, and the hero has to choose. When you get a home equity loan, you want to make sure you know enough not to choose the door with the tiger!

This book gives you the key to the correct door. The knowledge you will gain will keep you from opening the door to the tiger.

Your Home Is Your Castle

In general, your home represents a big part of you. It's not just a roof over your head. You've personalized it, you have memories in every room, and the psychological investment you probably have in it can be considerable.

There is the first problem. When you take out an equity loan, you are placing your home at risk. It is not some investment on a ledger sheet; it is your home. We can't emphasize this strongly enough. If you have trouble paying off this loan, the bank isn't going to repossess your car

---

* ABA 30-day delinquency rate for closed end second mortgages (1986).

or take away your TV; they're going to throw you out of your house. So tread carefully.

Your Home Is an Investment

Second, your home represents your largest single investment. Quite apart from whether you do or don't love your home, your home equity probably represents the bulk of your assets.

Prudent investment counselors will tell you to be conservative and adopt a maintenance position with the largest portion of your assets. You want to maintain the principal value to keep pace with inflation at little risk. If this were money, that would mean government bonds or an insured CD. Since this is real estate, appreciation alone will provide this for you, since appreciation generally runs between five percent and eight percent per year. You can add even more value, above market appreciation, if you add a garage, room, or deck. But the point is that you certainly don't want to do anything that will decrease the value of your house. And you certainly don't want to borrow on the equity in the house and then fritter away the money. Your home represents not only the fruits of your past labors but also, to a large extent, your future well-being. A misplaced choice can be disastrous. Again, tread carefully.

These are the two main considerations you need to think about before you even look at a home equity loan. And we can skillfully guide you through the quicksand of potential problems and mistakes. With this book, you will have all the knowledge at hand to make the right choice.

Why Should You Trust Us?

The question on your mind at this point is probably, "They talk a good line, but can they deliver?" Yes, we can. We teach the lenders how to design and make these loans. We know all the ins and outs of the various equity loans.

Whom have we taught? We have taught lenders at banks, savings and loans, credit unions and finance companies. We have been quoted extensively as experts on this subject by national publications. We have successfully authored a book on general bank pricing and profitability as well as another book teaching lenders how to make home equity loans.

The second good question would be, "Why are you bothering to do a book for consumers? Aren't you on the lenders' side?" Not necessarily. We're doing a book for consumers because it needs to be done. Our philosophy in working with lenders and financial institutions is that what's good for the customer will be good for the lender. Any loan product that's ill-conceived or provides undue risk to the customer is not advantageous to the lender either. Ultimately, when you take a close look at it, if you as the borrower fail and can't repay the loan, then the lender suffers also. This has proven to be true over the years with all types of lenders. Improper lending on the part of top management is normally the primary reason for the failure of a financial institution. If the lender takes care of you, then you will take care of the lender. There's no such thing as win/lose in a loan arrangement; for both sides it must be win/win.

In addition, there really aren't any books out there written by experts who know all the sides of this very complicated issue. We know not only the various products that can be offered, but also how to shop for them, what kinds of documents you will encounter, and all the different pricing factors you will see. And we can share this knowledge with you. A well-informed consumer is the best partner a successful banker can have.

What Is in This Book?

There is a lot in this book, and it's probably a good idea at this point to join us in a guided tour.

Chapter One you already know about. It's the gentle introduction you're reading right now.

Chapter Two discusses what a home equity loan is, how it came about and some of its history, a brief introduction to the various kinds of home equity loans and some of the purposes for getting a home equity loan.

Chapter Three is one of the harder chapters. There we tackle the tax issues. Uncle Sam in his infinite wisdom has offered an incentive for loans secured by real estate and a disincentive on any other type of consumer loan. We take a look at these tax advantages and describe what they mean to you. Be careful if you are considering an equity loan just for the tax aspects, because you may go through all the effort and expense of getting one only to find that the tax effect that you thought was there is not there. With the information presented in this chapter, you will be able to evaluate your own tax situation. And note that the tax aspects can be so complicated that not even the government, meaning the IRS, can figure them out. We discuss the Tax Reform Act of 1986 and subsequent changes to that Act passed by Congress in 1987 as part of the Budget Reconciliation Act. We cover the phase-in and phase-out of these laws and the effects on taxes depending on when the loan was taken out. This gets really complicated, so we provide numerous examples. We end the chapter with a feature you will see repeated throughout the book—a Strategies section to advise you as to what specific actions to take or choices to make.

Chapter Four discusses the closed end loan in detail. This loan is similar to the standard auto loan. This is the second mortgage loan that has been around for many years. Fixed rate loans are compared with variable rate loans, the various product features are discussed, and the advantages and disadvantages of this type of loan are laid out for you. And then we end with the Strategies section, advising you what to do.

Chapter Five covers the open end home equity loan, which is similar to a huge credit card. Much has been written about this type of loan in the press (some of it by the authors), and opinions have been stated ranging from that this is the greatest thing since sliced bread all the way to the loan is "poison." We will give you both sides of the story. The chapter again covers the fixed versus variable issues, although this section is shorter than the discussion in Chapter Four since it is very rare to find a fixed rate open end home equity loan. The various product features are discussed, and the advantages and disadvantages are presented. The chapter is ended with the now familiar Strategies section.

The day-to-day issues you will encounter if you get a home equity line of credit are discussed in Chapter Six. A line of credit has some unique features, such as the periodic drawing of funds, access devices, the billing statement, billing rights and disputes and other issues. These are all presented in this chapter.

Chapter Seven begins to address the question of pricing, an issue that is concluded in Chapter Eight. First, the most visible feature of pricing—APR—is explained. Fees are discussed, including application fees, points, closing costs, credit report fees, late fees, overlimit fees and annual fees. The trade-off between fees and rate is examined: which is better for you—higher fees and lower rate or lower fees and higher rate? Some variable-rate considerations that can affect the cost are discussed, such as indexing, negative amortization, and caps and floors. Finally, we advise you which choices are best for you in the Strategies section.

Other considerations that directly affect price are explained in Chapter Eight. Payment methods for both closed end and open end loans are discussed, including automatic debit. Credit insurance, which you are sure to encounter, is covered in all its fascinating detail. Whether you will be paying off your loan or rolling it over is addressed. And advice is offered in the Strategies section.

Chapter Nine examines the credit issue. How does a lender judge your credit? How do they decide how much they can lend you? A lender is primarily concerned with whether you will be paying the loan back in a timely manner. To assist in this judgment, they get an appraisal, they apply a loan to value ratio, and they look at the five C's of credit: capacity, character, collateral, capital and conditions. They also calculate the debt ratio to assist in setting the line size. They examine your past payment history. And then, once they have given you the loan, they do annual reviews. This chapter, in other words, takes the mystery out of credit analysis. You'll see there's no magic to it, just some commonsense formulas that lenders use to figure out what your house is worth and whether you can and want to pay the loan back. Maybe you can't do this like a lender does, but you can understand it. And finally, we suggest avenues you can take if your loan is denied.

Chapter Ten helps you shop for a home equity loan. Not all home equity loans are equal. Some are more advantageous than others, but to figure out which ones are best for you, you need to know the right questions to ask. We will take you through this process step-by-step and help you put together a comparison chart, so that when you call the lenders in your area you can get the right answers to guide you to the right decision. You will look at service, location, price and knowledge of product. Extensive examples are offered to show you how to compare lenders.

Loan closings are covered in Chapter Eleven. These can be scary and intimidating, even to those who know what to expect. You may remember what a loan closing was like, because you may recall the closing on your first mortgage. Closing on a home equity loan is simpler but still confusing. We discuss the various forms you will see and/or sign, including the forms you sign before the closing, at the closing, and after the closing. And we take you through the closing step-by-step so that you'll be prepared.

Finally, we hope you'll never have to read Chapter Twelve. This chapter covers what to do if you get in trouble with your loan. We discuss minor payment delays, such as late payments and dishonored payments. And then we get into the more serious problems and what sorts of actions the lender might take. The various events that could happen to cause the lender to take action are examined as well as what that action might be, such as calling the loan or offsetting other monetary assets. And finally the whole area of foreclosure is discussed, including going to court, the sheriff's sale, and the redemption period. And we don't leave you there; alternatives to foreclosure are presented, such as refinancing, deed-in-lieu and bankruptcy.

In the back of the book is included a Monthly Payment Calculator as an appendix. You can use this chart to calculate what your payments will be for various amounts that you could borrow at various interest rates. One of your primary concerns is probably, what will my monthly payment be? With the use of this chart, you can calculate the answer to that even before you start calling lenders to compare their various loan programs. We refer frequently to this chart throughout the book.

And there you have it. This is where we're headed. We hope you'll come along with us. The journey will be educational as well as, we hope, fun.

Chapter Two

What Is a Home Equity Loan?

Home equity loans are not new. They date back to the horse-and-buggy days and were called second mortgages. During the late 1800s, they were used by consumers to actually purchase their properties. Building and loan societies were the primary providers of first mortgage loans, and they usually required a 50 percent or 60 percent down payment. In addition, the loan term was generally limited to five or six years. To keep payment levels manageable, a balloon payment was then required at the end of the term.

Because of this unfavorable style of financing, many home buyers needed a second mortgage loan to help cover the down payment. But with the Great Depression of the 1930s and the resulting hard economic times, people lost their homes by the thousands. Many of these borrowed that 50 percent or 60 percent down payment, and their houses were highly leveraged. Thus, second mortgage loans and foreclosures became firmly intertwined in the minds of consumers. It was during this time that a stigma became attached to second mortgage loans. And this stigma stayed with consumers until the 1950s.

At the end of World War II, returning veterans had a huge appetite for housing, and this market demand spurred the evolution of the second mortgage loan from a very restrictive loan with a poor image into a flexible, affordable and popular loan. New housing construction was in great demand, and the housing industry was at an all-time high. Under the GI Bill, Veteran Administration (VA) loans were being offered for 15-year terms with no down payment. This changed the face of the standard first mortgage forever. And that directly affected second mortgages. The stage was set for the late 1950s when this housing stock was getting to be ten years old. Many of the veterans and others who owned these houses wanted to improve them by adding additional living space, such as patios or other amenities. And these homeowners, in the stable economic times of the '50s, had not only the desire to improve their homes but also the financial capabilities of supporting home improvement type loans.

Responding to this need for home improvement, the Federal Housing Authority created the FHA Title I Home Improvement Loan. This loan, although limited in the amount of money that could be borrowed, did allow homeowners to borrow 100 percent of their equity for home improvement and did allow terms of up to 15 years. Now second mortages once again became socially acceptable if the purpose was to improve the home. The FHA Title I program coupled with the consumers' desire for home improvements gave the second mortgage some renewed degree of popularity. But it still carried some of the original stigma it had developed during the Great Depression and people still avoided getting one if they could.

The next step in improving the acceptability of second mortgages came in 1974 when national banks were granted the authority to secure loans with second liens on real estate. This allowed the banks to work hand in hand with remodeling contractors in providing financing on home improvements. And in 1982, savings and loans were granted the power to offer second mortgage loans other than FHA Title I Home Improvement Loans.

During the 1980s, homeowners began to look at their houses in a slightly different light. They began to realize that their home was a major investment, in fact *the* major investment. As substantial equity began to be built up both by paying down the mortgage and through appreciation of housing stock in the marketplace, homeowners found that they could leverage themselves by borrowing on their homes' equity through second mortgages and use this money for a variety of purposes such as home improvement or education.

During this period, from the turn of the century through the 1970s, the standard second mortgage type was the fixed rate loan with a stated term, for example, a 20-year second mortgage at seven percent. It was rare, if not impossible, to find any other type of second mortgage. It was only in more recent years that second mortgages could be found with a variable rate or a flexible term.

What Is a Home Equity Loan?

What exactly is a home equity loan? Well, first and foremost, it is a second mortgage. What does that mean? When you originally purchased your home, you probably went to a bank or a savings and loan to get the money to purchase your house. When the lender gave you the money, they made an agreement with you. In return for giving you the money, the lender was allowed to take a financial interest in your house. This is technically called a lien or a mortgage. This mortgage allows the lender to take your house away from you if you don't make the payments on your loan. The lender wants more than just your word that you will pay them back. They want the right to come in and take your house and sell it to recover the money if you don't pay the loan back. Taking the house is called foreclosure. Foreclosures are more common with first mortgages than with seconds, but they do happen with seconds as well.

A second mortgage is a second lien after the first. If you bought a house some time ago for $50,000, and you still have $25,000 outstanding on that first mortgage, you would then have $25,000 equity in your house. If, in addition, your house appreciated to $100,000, you would then have $75,000 equity in your house. This $75,000 can secure a second mortgage. But the lender of the outstanding $25,000 has the first right to your house. And they will always have the first right until you pay off that $25,000. If you don't make payments and the lenders foreclose and sell your house, the first mortgage holder will get fully paid off, and the second mortgage holder gets what's left over. That's what second position means.

The second mortgage holder can also initiate foreclosure action. But they still can only get what's left over after the first mortgage is paid off. We go into greater detail on that in Chapter Twelve.

You can have third, fourth, or fifth mortgages. There is no technical reason why you can't have any number of mortgages on your house. However, if the lenders foreclose, will there be any equity left to pay off the third mortgage holder? Or the fourth? Or the fifth? It's highly unlikely, at which point the lenders have to look to you directly to make the payments if you can. This is why lenders get very nervous about being in a third position. And, of course, all these mortgages get very expensive for you because you have to pay fees to get each one. Instead, a potential third mortgage lender might suggest that you borrow enough to pay off the second mortgage, thus allowing them to take over the second position.

So a second mortgage means that you are giving up your equity rights in your house to the amount of the second mortgage, and in return you receive either the cash or the rights to draw the cash (if it is a line of credit).

What Types of Home Equity Loans Are Offered?

Let's take a brief look at some of the home equity loans being offered in the market today. This will be only an overview because each of these types of loans is covered in great detail later on. In fact, an entire chapter is devoted to each of the two major types.

Open Versus Closed

All second mortage loans or home equity loans can be divided into two basic types: the closed end loan and the open end loan. A closed end loan is like a standard auto loan. For example, you may borrow $10,000 at, say, ten percent, to purchase a new car. The loan is set up for 48 months with set payments of $253.63 per month. So you would pay $253.63 per month every month for 48 months. At the end of 48 months the balance on your loan is zero. During that period of time, you've paid back not only the principal but also interest to repay the lender for the use of their money. So with a closed end loan you know the exact term of the loan and the exact price. It's called *closed end* because you can't borrow more money at a later date under the same loan.

The open end loan, on the other hand, can best be compared to a credit card. With a credit card, instead of receiving a lump sum dollar amount, you get what is called a *line*. So instead of receiving money at the time you sign the documentation, you receive the right to draw funds. You can exercise this right by either going to your lender and getting a cash advance or by writing a check on your line. You can usually take out as much as you want up to the line limit. For example, if your line is $15,000, you can continue to draw funds until you have borrowed

$15,000. Once you reach $15,000, you can't spend any more money unless you pay some off or increase the line amount. This type of loan is called *open end* because you can always go back in and draw out more money.

Fixed Versus Variable

Home equity loans can be divided into two additional basic types: fixed rate and variable rate. Both open and closed end loans can have either a fixed rate or a variable rate. Fixed rate means that the rate is set up front when you take out the loan and never changes throughout its life. Variable rate means that the rate will change sometime during the life of the loan. These two types of rates are discussed in detail in later chapters.

What Can I Use This Loan for?

Each type of loan has certain purposes for which it is best suited. You will pick a certain type of loan, maybe open end, maybe variable rate, depending upon what you want to use the home equity loan for. There are some smart uses for each type of loan and some uses that are not so smart. Let's take a look at some of these uses.

A poor choice for a home equity loan is anything frivolous. Remember, you're putting your house on the line, so don't use the equity for trivial purchases.

What do people use a home equity loan for? The chart on the next page shows some common purposes for a home equity loan as well as what percentage of people use each purpose.*

Let's take a look at some of these purposes in more detail.

Home Improvement

The number one purpose, for both open and closed end loans, is home improvement. And this is a smart use. Using a home equity loan for home improvement makes a lot of sense because it provides double value. First, you receive the value and pleasure of the improvement for yourself. Whether that improvement is a room addition or a deck, it will

* *Home Equity Loans II*, Market Facts, Inc., Chicago, and Moebs $ervices, Wadsworth, Illinois (1986).

	Line of Credit	*Closed End Loan*
Home improvement	51.5%	49.6%
Business	25.5	11.5
Bill consolidation	25.5	24.8
Buy car/truck/van	17.0	9.7
Education	6.4	2.7
Buy second home	4.3	4.4
Vacation	4.3	4.4
Other	34.0	25.7

normally be an improvement that enhances the liveability of your home. And secondly, you're improving the market value of your home. While you're using up some of your equity with the loan if you look at it from the balance sheet side, you are also increasing the market value of your investment.

However, not all types of improvements actually improve the value of your house. The improvement that adds the most value is one that increases or improves the home's living space. An example would be a room addition. This is an excellent value because it increases the size of the dwelling, and you would generally get close to a dollar-for-dollar return in equity against the use of the equity. Another example that brings in a high return is adding a garage if you don't already have one. Other popular improvements that add to the value of your home are upgrading a kitchen, upgrading bathrooms, adding a fireplace, or adding a recreation room in a basement. All of these items increase the market value of the residence.

Some "improvements" are really maintenance items, and these add little if any market value to a house. These include replacing a furnace, a water heater or a roof. Maintaining or replacing parts of the physical plant of the house, meaning such equipment as a furnace, plumbing, water heater, or structural components of the house, such as the roof or the walls, really does not add to the market value of the property. That's because it is expected that a house will have a roof that won't leak and a furnace that works. If they don't work, they will detract from the normal market value of the property, but if they do, they won't add to it. Even if you replace an old furnace with a better furnace, the marketplace may not recognize your effort with a higher value for your house.

However, these are not necessarily poor choices for a home equity loan. While adding value to a house is certainly worthwhile, so is maintaining the value of your asset. Therefore, in general, any type of home improvement is considered a smart use for a home equity loan.

Education

Most homeowners are fulfilling their "Great American Dream" by owning a home. But what is the second "Great American Dream"? This isn't a quiz, so we'll give you the answer. The second Great American Dream is to send your children to college. Now, the average cost of sending a child to your own state university is about $2,000 per year. If you're not a resident, the cost jumps to $5,000. The cost of sending a child to a good private university can be $12,000 per year. And that's just the tuition; you can double that for room and board. Now take out your checkbook. Write down the total cost of sending all your children to college for four years and subtract that amount from the current balance in your checkbook. If you're like us, it quickly becomes clear that you'll probably need some additional money for school.

A college education is very expensive, and its cost keeps rising. But home equity loans can be used to help send your children through college. Now, is this a smart use or not? Your children are part of your household, so what better use of the assets of the household is there than improving their lives. Second, you have been building up the equity in your home as an investment. This investment is the payoff for working so hard. And you built that investment in part for your children. So, after buying some goodies for yourself, use that investment for your children's education. The bottom line is that education is a smart use for a home equity line.

Business

It might surprise you that many individuals use the equity in their home for business purposes. The average homeowner tends to think of a home equity loan as a consumer loan rather than a commercial loan. But these small business owners have enough faith in their business venture and themselves to offset any risk to their home or the asset value of their real estate. These borrowers are also assuming that the return on the business venture, in other words the profit, will be greater than the cost of the loan.

Why do people use the equity in their homes for business? First, it can be difficult to get financing if you run your own small business. Unlike a Fortune 500 company, you can't go to a major money center bank, borrow millions of dollars, and set your own terms. In fact, even if you get a business loan, you will probably still be required to pledge your personal assets to back up the assets of the business. As long as you have to pledge your home anyway, you may as well take a personal second mortgage loan. In fact, the interest rate and fees would be lower than a business loan and the risk is no different.

Using your home's equity for business purposes is not easily categorized as a smart or poor choice. It could be either. Here's a story as an example. About five years ago, a man came to us to borrow some money while we were still lenders at a bank. This man and his family wanted a second mortgage loan for a side business, which would be to start a chicken farm in Wisconsin in partnership with a friend. The idea was to buy some Wisconsin farmland, build some chicken coops on it and raise some chickens. He took out a $25,000 second mortgage loan on his home to help finance his end of the business. Well, that winter was one of the coldest in recorded history. And instead of having a thriving chicken farm, they wound up with 40,000 frozen chickens. They couldn't even sell them to Col. Sanders, because the chickens still had feathers on them. The home ended up in foreclosure.

If you decide to invest in a business, make sure the risk is low enough that you're willing to gamble your home. Jackie Gleason as Ralph Cramden of "The Honeymooners" always had some surefire scheme to get rich quick. If you currently have a thriving business that has a very good return on investment, then you probably would be smart to use your home's equity as collateral for a business loan. However, if you have a Ralph Cramden-type get-rich-quick scheme, you better think twice, or three or four times, before risking your home.

Bill Consolidation

Bill consolidation is a very popular use for home equity loans. The homeowner takes out a home equity loan, uses the proceeds to pay off existing debts like credit cards, personal loans, and maybe even an auto loan, and then has only one monthly payment.

This use of a home equity loan achieves a number of things. First, the total monthly payment will be lower than the total of the monthly payments to the other creditors. Second, the interest rate will probably be lower. And third, and potentially most important, because of the Tax Reform Act, most consumer loan interest is no longer fully tax deductible; the interest on a home equity loan can be. So it appears that bill consolidation is a smart use for home equity loans.

However, this is one of those choices that can be so poor that it can be hazardous to your health, as you will find out when you read Chapter Twelve on getting into trouble. Most home equity loans that go into foreclosure were used for bill consolidation. Why? Because borrowers who aren't adept at using credit to begin with get in over their heads through the use of credit cards and personal loans. The home equity loan seems to be an "easy way out." After all the debts are paid off with the proceeds from the home equity loan, these borrowers repeat their initial mistakes by going back out and using the credit cards all over again, running up their debts back to where they were before. Now these borrowers have not only the credit cards to pay off but also the home equity loan. The total bills that have to be paid exceed the amount that the borrower is able to repay and the results are disasterous.

The only way consolidation works out well as a use for a home equity loan is if the old patterns of credit abuse are not repeated. How do you insure that you have "learned your lesson"? One way is to close all the credit card accounts when you pay them off. Cut the credit cards in half and request that your account be closed. Another way is to seek credit counseling. Many metropolitan areas have credit counseling centers run on a not-for-profit basis through church organizations or community groups. These can be an excellent source of advice if you keep running into problems with credit. Less desirable are credit counseling firms that charge you for their services or guarantee to reinstate a good credit rating for you. That's often done at your expense, because the charges are very high or they may not be able to fulfill the promises they make.

What is the bottom line on using a home equity loan for bill consolidation? Is it a smart or is it a poor choice? Generally it can be a real time bomb unless you are sure that you can break the credit abuse cycle. Then and only then can it be a smart way to take care of outstanding bills.

Purchase of Personal Property

Equity loans are sometimes used for the purchase of personal property, such as furniture, a car or perhaps a boat.

The main issue we would raise in using a home's equity for the purchase of a consumer good concerns the loan term. If you bought a car that has an estimated useful life of five years, after which time you would trade it in or sell it, then you shouldn't take out a loan for ten years to pay for that car. That's why conventional car loans rarely exceed five years. You should never take out a home equity loan, or any loan for that matter, which has a longer term than the value of whatever you're buying.

Another caution when using home equity loans for purchase of consumer goods is—don't buy a toy. This falls into the frivolous category. Be careful about buying a second car you may not really need, or a boat or an RV. You may be tempted into buying a sports car you can't really afford, but since you can stretch the payments over ten or fifteen years, you can afford the monthly payments. But don't do it. We offer our advice again—don't use your home's equity for a frivilous purpose. And don't use your home's equity as a way to extend payments over a longer term than the value of the item you are purchasing.

So is it smart or not so smart to use your home's equity for the purchase of a consumer good? This use shares some characteristics with bill consolidation. If you can handle credit responsibly and if you can police yourself, it can be a smart use. If you use a home equity loan to buy a car rather than using a conventional car loan, you will be able to continue to deduct the interest. But if you make the home equity loan term longer than the estimated useful life of the item you are purchasing or if you buy a toy, these are poor uses that can easily get you in trouble.

In general, be careful what you use a home equity loan for. Use this book as a guide to the various kinds of home equity loans and what they can be used for. Tread carefully because you're mortgaging your castle. Don't end up in the same position as the chicken farmer and have all your assets frozen!

Chapter Three

The IRS and Your Home Equity Loan

"Question: I took out an $80,000 mortgage to buy a house for $100,000 in 1980. In January 1987, the house was reappraised for $125,000. The loan, which had been paid down to $75,000, was refinanced so that it totaled $110,000. After paying off the first loan, I used $5,000 of the proceeds for home improvement and $30,000 for a new car. The average balance on the loan was $109,000 last year, and I paid $10,000 in interest. How much of the interest is deductible?

"What (The IRS) Should Have Said: You may deduct $9,600 as mortgage interest and $260 as personal interest. To arrive at that, use Form 8598 and multiply the amount of interest paid ($10,000) by the ratio of the qualified loan limit (in this case the home's purchase price plus improvements, or $105,000) to the average balance of the debt ($109,000). This produces deductible mortgage interest of $9,600 after rounding. The other $400 of interest paid is treated as personal interest, and 65 percent of it, or $260, can be deducted.

"What (The IRS) Did Say: An IRS woman in Des Moines, Iowa, said all the interest is fully deductible. At the Denver office, a woman said that the portion used to buy the car couldn't be deducted at all and that the rest would be partly deductible as personal interest. The three other staffers said a portion couldn't be deducted, but only a man in Dallas correctly said that the limit would be based on the home's purchase price plus improvements. One employee directed the caller to an incorrect form."*

* "IRS Staffers Are Ready to Assist Taxpayers, but Not Always Able," *Wall Street Journal*, 18 February 1988.

If the government doesn't know what it is doing, how are you supposed to know? The Tax Reform Act of 1986 was supposed to simplify taxes and for the most part it did, but in the area of consumer interest deductions, there's mass confusion. With the additional rules passed by Congress on December 23, 1987, as part of the Budget Reconciliation Act, the whole area of interest deductibility for consumer loans and home mortgages is really a mess. This chapter will lead you through that mess.

What Happened to Consumer Interest?

For several years, Congress struggled with reforming the tax code, which was last done in the early '50s. One of the intentions of Congress in passing the Tax Reform Act, which completely rewrote the Internal Revenue Code, was to take incentives away from borrowers and give incentives to savers. The jury is still out as to whether or not it was successful. But one thing was clear. Interest on consumer loans could no longer be deducted on itemized tax forms. This interest deductibility would be phased out through 1991. Shown in Table 3-1 are the percentages of interest that can be deducted starting in 1987 until complete phaseout in 1991. For example, in 1987, only 65 percent of the interest on a consumer loan would be deductible on itemized tax returns.

Here's an example of how this will affect you. Assume that on

Table 3-1
Percent Allowable Deduction
for Consumer Loans
Under the Tax Reform Act of 1986

Tax Year	*Percent Allowed*
1987	65%
1988	40%
1989	20%
1990	10%
1991	0%

Table 3-2
1987 New Car Loan
$10,000 @ 10% for 48 Months

	Interest Paid	*Tax Deductible*	*Not Tax Deductible*
1987	$903.69	$587.40	$316.29
1988	679.62	271.85	407.77
1989	432.09	86.42	345.67
1990	158.64	15.86	142.78
Total	$2,174.04	$961.53	$1,212.51
Times Maximum Tax Rate of 28% =	$608.73	$269.23	$339.50

January 1, 1987, you bought a new car. You got a $10,000 loan at ten percent for 48 months. Shown in Table 3-2 is the interest you would pay on $10,000 for each of the four years that the loan would be outstanding from 1987 through 1990. You know from Table 3-1 that the allowable interest deduction is 65 percent in 1987, 40 percent in 1988, 20 percent in 1989 and ten percent in 1990. Now multiply those percentages by the amount of interest paid, and the result is the second column—the tax deductible portion of the interest. The third column is, of course, the non-tax deductible portion.

You would pay a total of $2,174.04 interest on the $10,000. Over the four years, only $961.53 is tax deductible, while $1,212.51 can't be deducted. If you were paying taxes at the maximum tax rate of 28 percent, itemizing interest paid would normally allow you to deduct 28 percent of the total interest paid, for a direct reduction of your taxes owed of $608.73. However, under the new rules, you can only deduct 28 percent of $961.53, or $269.23; you have to pay $339.50 more taxes because that's the amount that you can't deduct.

What about Interest on Real Estate Loans?

But you do have an alternative. Tables 3-1 and 3-2 apply only to interest on *consumer loans.* They don't apply to interest on loans *secured by real estate.* Interest on loans secured by real estate is still fully deductible. That's the key point, and that's why you bought this book.

If you're deciding whether to get a home equity loan primarily to preserve interest deductibility, the $339.50 in Table 3-2 is the number you have to look at. Will your home equity loan cost you more than $339.50 to obtain? In most cases, it probably would. So, in 1987 it was probably not worthwhile for you to go out and get a home equity loan. You would have paid more in title fees, appraisals, closing costs, application fees and other fees than you would have gained as a tax benefit. In addition, you might have had to pay a higher interest rate on the home equity loan than the ten percent you could have gotten on the car loan.

But in Table 3-3 we move forward a year. In 1988 it might be worthwhile to get a home equity loan under this example. Table 3-3 uses

Table 3-3
1988 New Car Loan
$10,000 @ 10% for 48 Months

	Interest Paid	*Tax Deductible*	*Not Tax Deductible*
1988	$903.69	$361.48	$542.21
1989	679.62	135.92	543.70
1990	432.09	43.21	388.88
1991	158.64	0.00	158.64
Total	$2,174.04	$540.61	$1,633.43
Times Maximum Tax Rate of 28% =	$608.73	$151.37	$457.36

the same example as Table 3-2: a $10,000 loan is taken out at the beginning of the year at 10 percent for 48 months. Of course, the same phaseout is in effect, but since the loan starts in 1988 rather than 1987, even less of the interest over the life of the loan is deductible. In total, then, you can only deduct $540.61 over the life of the loan. Times a tax rate of 28 percent, the tax benefit is only $151.37. Now the key figure to look at is the $457.36 you can't deduct. Can you get a home equity loan with lower fees than $457 for the same ten percent interest rate? Probably. With a lot of the artificial incentive and teaser rates that have come out of Detroit, it might still be beneficial for you to stick with the auto loan and forego the interest deductibility, but you can see how the decision is made.

This, then, is a simplified presentation of the net effect of the various laws. But now we have to get into more detail. Stick with us; this can be interesting in more ways than just deductibility.

The Tax Reform Act of 1986

When the Tax Reform Act was passed, it created various laws which went into effect on August 17, 1986. These same laws were modified after October 13, 1987, as part of the Budget Reconciliation Act which was signed on December 23, 1987. So a period of 14 months exists, from August 17, 1986 to October 13, 1987, in which the original provisions on home equity loans from the Tax Reform Act apply. After that, on October 14, 1987, new provisions are in effect.

One of the provisions of the Tax Reform Act, as already stated, was that interest on consumer loans was no longer tax deductible. However, interest on first mortgage loans or any loan secured by real estate—that is, using real estate as the collateral—would still be tax deductible.

Of course, Congress is not going to give you a benefit like this without lots of rules. And it is primarily these rules that make this law so complicated.

The first major rule has to do with the amount that can be borrowed on which interest is deductible. You can, of course, borrow any amount you and the lender agree on, but there is a limit on how much of the loan you can deduct interest. This limit was the lower *of the fair market value of the house* or *the original purchase price plus improvements.* So whichever one of these two amounts, fair market value or purchase price plus improvements, was lower, that was how much you could borrow on which you could deduct the interest. In addition, any indebtedness from prior loans secured with the same real estate had to be subtracted from whichever of the two amounts you used.

All of this is probably confusing, so let's take a look at some examples. In Table 3-4 are shown the loanable amounts that might be taken out under two examples. In the first example, the fair market value of the house is determined to be $110,000. The original cost was $50,000 and the outstanding first mortgage is $30,000. Following the rule of the lower of fair market value or original purchase price or cost, the $50,000 of original cost is the limit because it is lower than fair market value. From that, the first mortgage must be subtracted, which is $30,000. This results in a total possible home equity loan of $20,000 on which interest is deductible. This is a significant calculation because a lot of people think that the appreciation in their home, under the old tax law, can be used. But when they sat down to do their taxes for 1987, they found that this wasn't the case and they couldn't deduct all the interest.

In the second example shown in Table 3-4, the original cost remains the same, at $50,000. But now the fair market value of the house is $40,000. Housing market values can decrease below cost. Current examples would be depressed areas of the country, like the Dakotas, the upper Midwest, the Southwest, or parts of the West. Now, applying the same rule of the lower of fair market value or original cost or purchase price, you have to choose the fair market value of $40,000. Subtracting

Table 3-4
Loanable Amounts

	1st	*2nd*
Fair Market Value	$110,000	$40,000
Original Cost	50,000	50,000
First Mortgage Outstanding	30,000	30,000
Home Equity	20,000	10,000

the first mortgage outstanding of $30,000 would produce a maximum home equity loan with deductible interest of $10,000.

Note that the purchase price or cost of a home can be increased by home improvements. Technically, a tax advisor would call this total the *basis* of the home's value. A critical question is, what is a home improvement? This is an area of the tax law that is very gray.

Over the years there have been cases establishing precedence as to what home improvements are, but for the most part the IRS has not defined this explicitly. The major guideline appears to be value. If a home improvement adds value to the house, then it increases the purchase price or the basis. But what adds value? Maintenance items do not add value. So adding a new roof to the house, painting, replacing a furnace, these do not add value. However, landscaping, adding a deck, adding a room addition, adding a garage, these all add value to the property and therefore would increase the price or basis of the home.

Some items that look like maintenance can add value. For example, if you replace the roof on your home with different types of shingles, let's say an insulated energy-saving variety different from the original shingles that were on the roof, this would add value to the home and the material could be added to the basis of the home.

The original Tax Reform Act also allowed that the purchase price plus improvements could be exceeded for some specific purposes, basically education and medical expenses. For example, say your daughter has just graduated from high school and has been admitted to an accredited massage school. You need to come up with money for her tuition, and you want to use a home equity loan to do it. However, your original first mortgage and another home equity loan already equal your purchase price plus improvements. The original Tax Reform Act allows you to get another home equity loan that would exceed the purchase price plus improvements as long as it does not exceed the fair market value and is used for education or medical purposes. You can still get an interest deduction for the amount that you borrowed on your home equity loan, and your daughter can go to massage school.

These are the basic provisions of the original laws pertaining to the non-deductibility of consumer loan interest and the deductibility of interest tied to a loan secured by real estate.

But now the new law comes along and changes things.

The New Law

Congress saw several things happening in the marketplace because of its original provisions for the deductibility for consumer interest. First, it found that taxpayers were deducting interest on loans that were used for other things than acquisition or improvement of a residence. Congress' intent was that only interest on loans for the acquisition or improvement of a residence or for education or medical expenses could be deducted. But this restriction was being bypassed, and taxpayers were getting home equity loans for other purposes.

Second, significant amounts of borrowing were being done under home equity loans. The Federal Reserve started to track the amount of home equity loans that were actually being booked by lenders. Thousands of executives at financial institutions flocked to training programs to find out how to do home equity loans. Literally, billions of dollars of home equity loans were added to the books of lenders around the country.

Third and most important, Congress saw that the present law was needlessly complex. Trying to understand fair market value and the purchase price plus improvements and figuring out how to get this across to the taxpayer was difficult. The IRS was faced with a myriad of options that it would have to report and regulate, and Congress felt that the whole process was too difficult for the average taxpayer.

Finally, Congress had originally intended that two residences could be used as collateral on a real estate or home equity loan. These could be a person's principal residence plus a second home, such as a summer home. Many consumers viewed their mobile homes, recreational vehicles (RVs), and even boats as a second home, and tried to pledge these as a second residence in order to preserve the interest deductibility on mobile home, RV, and boat loans. Congress felt that this was a misuse of the law.

To try to address these problems, Congress enacted the Budget Reconciliation Act which President Reagan signed into law on December 23, 1987. This Act contained some new provisions for home equity loans.

First, for home equity loans made on or after October 14, 1987, the limits, restrictions and other provisions would be simplified from the original law. This created a period of time from August 17, 1986, through October 13, 1987, during which the original provisions were grandfathered. Why was this done? Well, some taxpayers could benefit from the original provisions. Taxpayers who had recently purchased expensive homes and also had put down a large downpayment could potentially get a bigger loan on which the interest would be deductible than they could under the new provisions. So the grandfathering provisions were important to those who took out a loan between August 17, 1986, and October 13, 1987.

Differences From the Old Law

The new law said that home equity loans on which interest is deductible would be limited to $100,000. In addition, the loan to acquire the real estate, usually the original first mortgage, had a limit of $1,000,000. The law calls this *acquisition indebtedness*. Although this second limitation of acqusition debt doesn't affect most Americans, Congress included it because it felt that there were a large number of rich Americans who were buying huge, expensive homes and still being able to deduct the interest. It felt that these individuals should not have these interest deductions, and so it limited the amount that could be borrowed on a mortgage to purchase the property to $1,000,000. Congress made it even clearer, stating that homeowners could borrow $1,000,000 on the original acquisition of their home and get a home equity loan for $100,000 for a total of $1.1 million on which the interest would be deductible.

The $100,000 limitation had no special purpose restriction. So taxpayers could use this amount for any purpose they wanted. They could use the money to buy a boat, go on a vacation, add an addition to the house, use it for education, whatever they wanted. Up to $100,000, they could deduct all the interest.

The fair market value limitations still applied, however. Loans that were secured with real estate could not exceed the fair market value of the property. So now the "lower of" rule is restated as the *lower of fair market value* or *$100,000*. In addition, the amount of the home equity loan that could be taken out was calculated to be the fair market value of the property minus any indebtedness currently on the property. Congress did not want individuals to take out one loan after another, secure it with their property, exceed the fair market value of the property, and never deduct outstanding loans.

Congress also specifically eliminated any special provisions for education and medical expenses for loans booked after October 13, 1987. Since a high limit of $100,000 was allowed, it felt individuals could use the money for any purpose.

Finally, Congress had also observed that some individuals were refinancing their first mortgage, getting additional money from that refinancing over and above what they owed, using those additional funds for various purposes, and still deducting the interest. To eliminate this possibility, Congress put in a special rule, as follows: on a refinancing you cannot exceed your current level of debt. For example, if your outstanding first mortgage is $43,000 and you were to refinance your first mortgage but were able to get more, say $50,000, you could only deduct the interest on the $43,000. If you wanted also to deduct the interest on the additional $7,000, that $7,000 would have to be a second mortgage, not part of the first. Then, as long as the total financing on the residence didn't exceed $100,000, you would be able to deduct all the interest.

Common Provisions

Between the two laws, what we're calling the old law or original Tax Reform Act which started in August of 1986, and what we are calling the new law which started on October 14, 1987, there are some common provisions.

Fair Market Value

It is common to both laws that taxpayers have to consider the fair market value of the property every year whether they're using the old or the new law. Take a look at Table 3-4 again. Instead of being two different residences, assume that the examples here are the first year and the second year for the same residence. In the first year, you take out a home equity loan for $20,000. Since you get the loan before the new law goes into effect, you are allowed to deduct the interest on the entire $20,000. But suppose you live in an area where the major industry is oil.

The price of oil falls, companies in your area start laying off thousands of employees, and the general economic climate of your town goes into a tailspin. And the market value on your $110,000 home plummets to $40,000.

The big question is what happens to your home equity loan in the second year? The rule is the lower of fair market value or purchase price, or the lower of fair market value or $100,000, depending on when the loan was booked. If the home equity loan was booked before October 13, 1987, the debt is grandfathered and you can still deduct the interest on the full $20,000. But if the loan was booked on or after October 14, 1987, the new law applies. Since fair market value is below $100,000, you must use the fair market value as the basis for your tax calculations. After subtracting the outstanding mortgage, you are only allowed a $10,000 home equity loan and so only the interest on $10,000 is deductible.

How is the IRS going to police this? At the present time, no one knows. Taxpayers have to fill out form 2119 when they sell their home which shows the original purchase price and the price they are selling the home for. When this form is filled out, the IRS could go back to previous returns and detect that you indicated a higher fair market value than the house had in the second year. Therefore, you deducted interest when you shouldn't have, and the IRS may penalize you. So it would be to your benefit to keep track of the fair market value of your home.

How can you track fair market value unless you sell your house? Actually, it's not as hard as you may think. Neighbors talk, homes are sold, and via the "community grapevine" you can get a fairly good feel for the rising or falling values in your particular community or neighborhood. The real danger is that values may fall lower than the total indebtedness that you have secured by the property. Not only is this bad for tax purposes but also for you financially because you end up owing the bank more than the home is worth.

Two Residences

A second area that is common to both tax laws, as we mentioned earlier, is that two residences could be used. Under the old law, many people classified their mobile home, RV, or boat as a second residence. When Congress reexamined the law for potential changes, it planned to specifically disallow the use of mobile homes, RVs, and boats as second residences. However, in the final vote on the new law, these particular provisions were thrown out. It appears that Congress caved in at the last minute to specific lobbying groups and left this area gray, which means it's in the hands of the IRS.

However, take a look at the intent of Congress. The intent of the law is to restrict interest deductibility to loans on *living quarters*. If your RV is truly a recreational vehicle and not your living quarters, then don't try to make a case to deduct the interest on the loan for your RV. However, if you are a retired taxpayer and you have an RV in which you drive to warmer climates in the winter and then live in it during the winter, this is truly a second home. Therefore any interest on a loan for this RV would legitimately be tax deductible. Once again, it is the intent.

Unlimited Liens

Allowed under both sets of tax provisions are an unlimited number of liens that you can put on your property. You could have a first mortgage, a second mortgage, a third mortgage, even a fourth mortgage. As long as you don't exceed the specific provisions under either set of laws, you can have as many liens as lenders allow. But that's the real restriction. Lenders don't like being in a third, fourth, or fifth position on a property; it's not very secure. You'll find very few lenders who will do that type of lending. So in this case limitations are placed on what you can do by the marketplace, rather than by Congress, which is the way it works best anyway.

Since we're on the subject of liens, some lenders will do a home equity or second mortgage on your home, but they'll want other collateral in addition. For example, you may want to borrow money for the purchase of an automobile. The lender may have you sign a second mortgage and then take the title to your car in addition to the security interest in your house. If you default or don't make payments, the lender will probably come after the car because that's the easier collateral to repossess and resell. The only reason you signed the mortgage is to allow you to preserve the interest deductibility on the auto loan. We advise against this approach. Although it may seem tempting, this is circumventing the intent of the tax law, and the IRS frowns on this kind of tax avoidance.

Alternative Minimum Tax

Another provision of the tax law pertains to the Alternative Minimum Tax. This is a law that has been with us since 1978 when another revision of the tax laws was made. Basically, the Alternative Minimum Tax law says that everybody must pay something. The law is aimed at the rich, who, through investments and tax loopholes, can avoid paying any tax. The Alternative Minimum Tax eliminates loopholes and various deductions, with the bottom line being that you do pay some tax, no matter how many tax deductions you have. One of the items that is included in the calculation of the Alternative Minimum Tax is interest on consumer loans that were not intended for original construction or purchase of *one* residence. So even if you have a home equity loan, if you are subject to the Alternative Minimum Tax, then you may lose the interest deductibility of the home equity loan.

How do you know if you're subject to the Alternative Minimum Tax? The best way is to consult your tax advisor, but as a rule of thumb, if your household is making $50,000 or more of gross income, you stand a good chance of being subject to the Alternative Minimum Tax. In addition, if you have investments such as oil and gas, cattle feeding lots, apartment buildings, or the like, then you will be subject to the Alternative Minimum Tax. It is very important that you consult your tax advisor if you are a maximum tax rate payer before you get a home equity loan.

Remember, *you*, not the lender, are responsible for compliance with the tax laws. Some taxpayers may rely on the assumption that their friendly, knowledgeable lender would never give them a loan that would exceed the IRS guidelines. If you believe this, you should talk with us, because we have some land in Florida you may be interested in buying! *You* are responsible because *you* sign the tax return. Don't be misled by what a lender may or may not tell you in this area.

Maximum Loanable Amount

You may be confused by what the lender tells you and by the tax laws regarding how much you can borrow. Some examples of the old law and the new law may clarify matters.

Shown in Table 3-5 is the maximum loanable amounts from three perspectives. In the first column, the tax policy under the Tax Reform Act of 1986 is applied. In the second column, the new tax policy which became effective after October 13, 1987, governs. And in the final column is the underwriting or loan policy of most institutions. Assume the fair market value of your home is $110,000. In general, a lender will lend 80 percent of that fair market value (FMV), or a total of $88,000. Also assume your original purchase price was $75,000 and you made improvements of $20,000. Finally, the outstanding amount of your first mortgage is $58,000. All these figures are the same in all three examples.

Table 3-5
Maximum Loanable Amount

	Tax Policy TRA 1986	*Tax Policy 10/14/87*	*Lenders' Policy*
Fair Market Value	$110,000	$110,000	$110,000
80% times FMV	88,000	88,000	88,000
Purchase Price	75,000	75,000	75,000
Improvements	20,000	20,000	20,000
1st Mortgage Balance	58,000	58,000	58,000
Loanable Amount	$37,000	$42,000	$30,000

Under the tax policy of the Tax Reform Act, the limit on amount borrowed is the lower of fair market value or the original purchase price plus improvements, so that limit would be the $95,000 of purchase price plus improvements. From this $95,000 is subtracted the outstanding first mortgage for a loanable amount of $37,000, all of the interest of which would be deductible.

Under the new tax policy which went into effect on October 14, you are now limited to the fair market value or $100,000, so the limit would be $100,000. After subtracting the $58,000 of the first mortgage, the maximum loanable amount is $42,000, all of the interest of which would be tax deductible.

But is this what you can really borrow? Will you be able to find a lender that will lend you either $37,000 under the old law or $42,000 under the new law? No, you won't. Why? The lender's policy is to take 80 percent of your fair market value, or $88,000, and subtract the amount of your first mortgage from that. So $88,000 less $58,000 calculates to a maximum loanable amount of $30,000. You might be able to find a lender that would allow a higher loan-to-value ratio than 80 percent, but probably not. Just remember, ultimately *you are responsible!*

Strategies

Congress has complicated interest deductibility to the point of exasperation. We hope that we have led you through this maze so that you now have a better understanding.

There are a few things to remember before you get your home equity loan. First, recognize that these provisions pertain only to people who itemize deductions. Shown in Table 3-6 are Internal Revenue Service statistics for 1983 which show the total number of returns filed and the percentage of those returns that itemized deductions. Then the itemized deductions that included interest deductions are listed. Note that only one-third of Americans used interest as an itemized deduction. So approximately two out three Americans aren't using interest as a deduction, most of them because they don't itemize. If you don't itemize, then a home equity loan loses a major advantage for you

Table 3-6
Income Tax Return Statistics*

Total Returns Filed	96,321,310
Returns with Itemized Deductions	35,230,292 - 37%
Returns with Interest Deductions	31,683,573 - 33%

* Individual Income Tax Returns, Statistics of Income, Internal Revenue Service, 1983.

because you can't list the interest as a deduction. So you might as well go out and get an automobile loan or a credit card loan if the interest rates are comparable, because you're not itemizing anyway.

If a lender offers to make you a car loan and wants to take both the car and your house as collateral under the guise of a home equity loan, beat a hasty exit from that institution. This is not good lending, and it's not good for you. It's not good for you because you're giving a lot of security for one loan. It's not good for the lender because they are doing it to assist you to circumvent the tax laws. This borders on tax evasion, not tax avoidance. If you get questioned, the IRS might say that you're trying to circumvent Congress' intent. The bottom line concerning the use of multiple collateral is, *don't do it,* because eventually the IRS will probably issue a ruling or go to court with some taxpayer, hopefully not you, and eliminate this particular loophole.

Finally, if you're confused by this chapter or you just don't like dealing with taxes at all, consult a tax advisor. Even if you aren't confused and even if you do like taxes, we strongly urge you to consult your tax advisor before getting a home equity loan.

Home equity loans are not for everyone. Choose wisely and consult your financial advisors before you get one.

Chapter Four

The Closed End Home Equity Loan

Home equity loans can be divided into two types—closed end and open end. The closed end loan has always been a standard of the lending industry and is familiar to most consumers, so let's start with this loan first.

What Is a Closed End Home Equity Loan?

The closed end loan is sometimes called the "plain vanilla closed end" loan because it's the most common loan type encountered by consumers. A good example of a closed end loan is an automobile loan. Keep the standard auto loan in mind as we examine closed end loans. In a closed end loan, the *end* or the term is fixed. Within that term, you will fully repay all the principal that you borrowed and all the interest that has been charged on that principal. For example, if you borrowed $10,000 for an automobile for a term of 48 months, then you would repay the full amount of the principal and the interest charged over the 48 months or four years. It is called a closed end loan, because, once you actually receive the funds, your ability to borrow more is gone; the term is fixed or *closed*. The loan has a set term or time period during which the loan would be fully paid off, so the end or term is said to be closed. If you wanted to borrow more money in the middle of a 48-month closed end auto loan, you would have to refinance this closed end loan (meaning you would restructure or redo a new loan for the whole amount) or you would have to borrow the additional funds by getting another loan.

The significant features of this loan are:

(1) The loan is simple in concept, and it is understood by most consumers seeking to borrow money;

(2) All the money is received in one lump sum up front at the beginning of the loan term (at *origination*);

(3) By the end of the loan term, the entire loan plus interest is repaid;

(4) No further money can be borrowed during the term of that specific loan, unless you get a whole new loan.

Fixed Rate Versus Variable Rate

For most of the history of second mortgage lending, the loan of choice was fixed rate. This was true from the beginning when second mortgages were used to help finance down payments to buy homes, through the economic hardships of the 1930s when second mortgages often led to foreclosures, and finally into the revival of second mortgages when they were used for home improvements in the 1970s and early 1980s. This fixed rate home equity loan, offered by financial institutions almost to the exclusion of any other type, had a rate that was fixed for the life of the loan. This is still the most common type of loan, and in many ways it is still the most desirable. It is your standard plain vanilla second mortgage loan.

Fixed Rate

The fixed rate loan has a rate that doesn't change during the life of the loan. This provides a high degree of security for homeowners because they always know what their payments will be. For example, if you decide to add that deck to the back of your house, you'll know exactly what that home improvement will cost you per month for the entire life of the loan.

Many consumers prefer to relate to a monthly payment amount rather than to the total amount of the loan, because it's easier to budget a monthly amount. Also, value perceptions are easier when dealing with a monthly amount. For example, sitting on your new deck with family and friends needs to be worth the $3,500 plus the $900 in interest that it cost you. But sometimes totals are tough to put into perspective. If you consider instead that you'll have to pay back $106 a month for 42 months, you may find it's easier to decide whether that expenditure is worth it to you. It's always a good idea to look at not only the total amount of the loan plus interest but also the monthly payment. And with a fixed rate loan, that monthly payment will be the same for the entire term of the loan or 42 months in our example.

Another way to look at a fixed rate loan is that the consumer is saying, "I won't take any of the risk of a change in interest rates." So the risk of interest rate changes rests with the lender. If interest rates go up, you don't care because your payment stays the same. If interest rates go down, you do suffer some risk because your payments will be higher than they would have been if you had gotten the loan more recently with a lower rate. But, if interest rates go down substantially, you can always refinance your second mortgage loan at the lower rate. There are advantages and disadvantages to refinancing, and you have to consider more than just the rates in order to determine whether it is to your advantage. For example, up-front fees and closing costs have to be considered. Chapter Eight covers the pros and cons of refinancing.

Primarily, you will always know what you owe every month with a fixed rate loan. The fixed rate loan is the most popular loan for second mortgages for this very good reason.

Variable Rate

Within the last ten years another type of closed end loan has surfaced—the variable rate loan. Like its cousin the variable rate first mortgage loan, a variable rate home equity loan has an interest rate that can vary over the life of the loan. Instead of borrowing $15,000 at perhaps ten percent for ten years, you now would borrow $15,000 for ten years, but the ten percent may only be good for a short time and is subject to change.

How would an increase in interest rates actually affect a variable rate loan? How much would your payments increase, if the rate on your loan goes up? If rates rise, that rate increase must be reflected in your loan somehow, and there are two primary ways this can be done. Either the monthly payment can increase or the term of the loan can be extended. Usually, the payment varies. How much does the payment vary? In other words, how dangerous is a variable rate loan? And should you regret not getting a fixed rate loan? Those are a lot of questions, but let's take a closer look because these points are important to you.

Table 4-1
Effect of Increasing Rate on Payment
Loan of $20,000 for 10 Years

Interest Rate	*Monthly Payment*	*Dollar Increase Of Payment Over Original*	*Percent Increase Of Payment Over Original*
9.5%	$258.80	$ 0.00	0.0%
10.5	269.87	11.07	4.3
11.5	281.19	22.39	8.7
12.5	292.75	33.95	13.1
13.5	304.55	45.75	17.7
14.5	316.57	57.77	22.3
15.5	328.82	70.02	27.1

Table 4-1 illustrates what can happen with a sample home equity loan of $20,000 with a term of ten years. This loan will fully amortize over the ten years, meaning that at the end of ten years you will have paid the loan down to zero. Therefore, the term can't be extended if rates increase; rather, the monthly payment will be increased to allow the loan to pay off in ten years.

In the example, the loan starts at an interest rate of 9.5 percent. At this rate, your monthly payments are $258.80 a month. Let's assume that the promissory note you signed stipulated that your rate would never increase more than six percent or that the loan had what is called a six percent lifetime cap. Your rate can therefore increase from the beginning rate of 9.5 percent to 15.5 percent. You may think that's not too bad, that six percent isn't too much. But look at what can happen. The first column of the table lists the actual interest rate of your loan. The next column lists what your monthly payment would be for that interest rate. The third column shows how much your payment has increased in dollars over your original payment level. And the fourth column shows how much your payment has increased as a percentage of your original payment level. Look at the last figure. Your payment has actually increased more than 27 percent! This table shows that what started out as a manageable $258.80 per month payment can rise to $328.82. Now do you still think that's not too bad?

Because of this risk of the unknown as to what payment amounts would be, variable rate loans are usually not as popular as fixed rate loans. When consumers take out a large second mortgage loan, it is understandable that they'll want to know what payment levels will be for the entire life of the loan.

In high rate environments, however, fixed rate loans may well be priced above the repayment ability of many people, so variable rate loans become more acceptable. It is normal to see a spread between the fixed rate and the variable rate loans of about 1.5 percent to two percent. In other words, if the fixed rate loan is 11 percent, then you would probably be able to get a variable rate loan at nine percent or 9.5 percent. Looking at it from the lenders' side, they want to share the interest rate risk with you and will give you a break in price if you agree.

Caps and Floors. Caps are a good way to protect yourself against unmanageably high interest rates. A cap is the maximum percentage by which a rate can increase. Floors are a way for lenders to protect themselves against unmanageably low interest rates. A floor is the maximum percentage by which a rate can decrease.

When you shop for variable rate closed end loans, make sure to ask about caps and floors. All institutions do have caps and they must tell you what the cap is. That's a nice safety feature for you.

Caps and floors are discussed in detail in Chapter Seven.

Indexing. Variable rates are usually tied to an index, which is an independent rate upon which changes in your loan rate are based. Indexes can be prime rate, Treasury bill rate, Federal Home Loan Bank cost of funds rate or some other rate. Which rate is chosen should be of particular interest to you, and you should pay close attention when the lender explains the index to which your variable rate loan is tied. Some lending officers may not be familiar with the specifics of the index, but you should insist on having it explained to you. The choice of index can have a significant impact on the cost of your loan.

Indexing is explained in detail in Chapter Seven, including the pros and cons of the various index options.

A final danger of variable rate lending is something called negative amortization, where you can end up owing more than you originally borrowed because of high interest rates. You should discuss this with the lender and perhaps review the concept by reading Chapter Seven before you accept a variable rate loan.

Frequency of Rate Change. When comparing rate indexes, you need to be concerned with how often the rate changes. Frequency of rate changes can make a significant difference in the amount of your monthly payment. In a rising rate environment, it would be to your advantage to have your rate tied to an index that changes as infrequently as possible, such as every six months or once a year, whereas if rates are coming down you would want your rate to change every month. You can find a variety of options here, ranging from monthly rate changes to yearly, and occasionally you may find a lender offering a program where the rate changes once every three years.

Your rate may not change at predetermined times but rather whenever the index to which it is tied changes. Therefore, if your index remains the same, then your rate would not change. But if your index changes mid-month, then your rate changes. So your rate would change as many times as the index changes. If your rate does change, that rate change must be reflected in your payments somehow. How rate change is handled is discussed in Chapter Eight.

Which Rate Type Should You Choose?

There are advantages and disadvantages regardless of which rate type you choose.

Fixed rate loans allow you to know with certainty what your rate is and what your monthly payments will be for the life of the loan. However, variable rate loans allow you to take advantage of decreasing interest rates and are usually priced less than a fixed rate loan. So it really comes down to personal preference. The authors published a survey in 1986 in association with Market Facts, Inc.,* on consumer preferences

---

* *Home Equity Loans II*, Market Facts, Inc., Chicago, and Moebs $ervices, Wadsworth, Illinois (1986).

regarding home equity lending. One question was whether consumers cared more about interest rate or monthly payments. And the respondents were split, half and half. Fixed monthly payments allow you to budget more easily and accurately. But if you feel rates are coming down, you may want to take the risk of a variable rate loan. In addition, if this is only a short term loan, for perhaps a couple of years, you may want to risk a variable rate since the up-front costs of this type of loan are normally lower. Points are often not charged, and fees can be lower.

Product Features

Other than interest rate, product features you need to consider for a closed end home equity loan would be term, amount and purpose.

Term

Look at this feature carefully since term has the greatest single impact on a home equity loan's true cost. When you choose a home equity loan, you will have to choose among a variety of terms. For example, if you want to borrow $10,000, do you want to repay it in three years or five years or ten years? The answer probably is that you would want to repay it as quickly as possible while staying within your budget.

The easiest way to see how maturity or term affects monthly payment and true cost to you is to use an example. Table 4-2 illustrates

Table 4-2
Effect of Term on Payment
Loan of $15,000 at 10%

Term	*Monthly Payment*	*Total Interest*
3 years	$484.01	$2,424.38
5 years	318.71	4,122.34
7 years	249.02	5,917.48
10 years	198.23	8,787.13
15 years	161.19	14,014.34

several different repayment options. You could refer to the Monthly Payment Calculator in the appendix at the back of the book and determine your own payments, but in this example we are doing the work for you. Why not? That's why we're here.

If you borrowed $15,000 at a fixed rate of ten percent and agreed to pay it back in three years, your monthly payment would be $484 plus a penny. And the total interest you would pay over the life of the loan would be $2,424.38. If $484 per month were too much for your budget, you might want to consider stretching out the loan over ten years. In this case, your monthly payments are cut by more than half to $198.23. That sounds wonderful. But now look at the total interest you pay for the privilege of this lower monthly payment. The total interest you are paying over the ten years is $8,787, more than 3.5 times the amount of interest you would have paid at 36 months! You might think that if you cut your payment in half, you would only increase your interest charges to twice as much. But no. You will more than double your interest expense. And if you were to extend the term to 15 years, your total interest payment would be almost equal to the loan itself. To take a less extreme example, look at the difference between the three-year loan and the five-year loan. The five-year loan will reduce your payment by 34 percent over the three-year loan, but the five-year loan costs 70 percent more in total interest.

The moral of Table 4-2 is that the reduction in monthly payments really costs you more in interest than what you can save in monthly payments. Your best bet is to always have the highest payment you can afford in order to shorten the term of the loan. The other side of that coin, however, is that you don't want to stretch yourself too much in making a high monthly payment. You always want to set your payment at an affordable level and at an amount you can cover should there be an interruption in your income for a month or two. You want to own the loan instead of having the loan own you.

If you want to make these same sort of calculations yourself, Table 4-3 gives you a format to use to figure out the optimal term in relation to the repayment and the interest amount for any loan you may be considering. Remember, the purpose of this exercise is to determine a payment that is affordable but also to pay the least amount of interest possible. Don't let the idea of a very low monthly payment lure you into

Table 4-3
Worksheet for Interest Calculation

Term (months)	x	*Payment*	=	*Total to Repay*	-	*Principal*	=	*Interest*
________	x	________	=	____________	-	________	=	_______
________	x	________	=	____________	-	________	=	_______
________	x	________	=	____________	-	________	=	_______
________	x	________	=	____________	-	________	=	_______
________	x	________	=	____________	-	________	=	_______
________	x	________	=	____________	-	________	=	_______
________	x	________	=	____________	-	________	=	_______

Example:

Term (months)	x	Payment	=	Total to Repay	-	Principal	=	Interest
60 mos	x	$318.75	=	$19,125	-	$15,000	=	$4,125

a term longer than you really need to repay the loan.

Here is how you can use this table. With the Monthly Payment Calculator table in the appendix, you first determine the monthly payment based on the amount of money you want to borrow and the suggested rate. You do this for the various terms you want to consider. So on the first five lines of column one of Table 4-3, you might write 48, 60, 72, 120 and 180. Then in the next column, write the payment you would have to pay every month for that term. You get this payment from the appendix. Once you have the term and the payment, you multiply the term in months times the payment to calculate the total amount that you will repay on this loan if you pay all the way to maturity. You then subtract from that the principal amount borrowed. And the difference is the total interest that you would pay over the term of the loan.

Let's do an example. Using a loan of $15,000 at an interest rate of ten percent, you can read in the appendix that a term of five years or 60 months results in a payment of $21.25 per thousand. In this case, since you are borrowing $15,000, you multiply the payment factor of $21.25 per thousand by 15 (15 x $1,000 = $15,000) to calculate a monthly payment of $318.75. So in column two, under *Payment,* you write $318.75. This payment is then multiplied by 60 months for the five-year term of the loan. This gives you a total loan repayment of $19,125. From that you subtract the principal of $15,000, and the remainder is the interest you would pay over the life of the loan—$4,125.

You then do this same exercise for the other terms you are considering, so you can compare whether a reduction in the monthly payment is worth the extra interest you have to pay. And only you can be the judge of that.

Principal Amount

The amount you borrow can range from a few thousand dollars up to the total equity in your house, which may be well over $100,000. With any home equity loan product, you normally will not want to borrow more than you need. Your real estate, especially the home in which you live, is probably the single largest investment you have. In addition, it's the roof over your head and perhaps the single greatest source of personal security. Because of this security aspect, there is an intangible nature to a home equity loan that cannot be measured in dollars. Your home is your castle to a very real extent and the culmination of "the great American dream." You shouldn't downplay this aspect. Realize its impact and don't borrow more than you need.

Purpose

There are a variety of worthwhile purposes for a home equity loan. And then there are some that aren't so worthwhile. The most common uses for a closed end loan (in the order of preference*) are home improvement or remodeling; bill consolidation; investment or business uses; purchase of other goods such as automobiles, recreational vehicles or boats; and education.

The single most popular purpose is for home improvement. This makes sense since many home improvements are quite expensive.

---

* *Home Equity Loans II,* Market Facts, Inc., Chicago, and Moebs $ervices, Wadsworth, Illinois (1986).

Room additions, garages or rehabilitation of kitchens or bathrooms can run into many thousands of dollars. A home improvement or an addition costing $40,000 or more is not unusual. Since the purpose enhances the value of the property, there is usually less reluctance to take a second mortgage for home improvements than for other purposes. It should be remembered, however, that no home improvement will add dollar-for-dollar value to the property. It is very unlikely that you will get back exactly what you've put into the house. Therefore, you should judge the worth of any home improvement by its intrinsic value to you as well.

Educational expenses are another common purpose for home equity loans because sending a son or daughter to four years of college today costs a lot. In fact, if owning a home is the great American dream, sending your son or daughter to college is the second great American dream. And using your home equity is an excellent funding source. Then all you need to do is to convince the student to pay you back after all that education has resulted in a great job. Good luck.

In addition, the use of an equity loan for purchase of such goods as an auto is becoming more common. This is a purpose, however, which lends itself more appropriately to the open end type of equity loan because of that loan's flexibility and greater likelihood of lower fees. This purpose is covered in detail in the next chapter.

Placing a second mortgage on your home for an investment is riskier. An example of this would be making a great buy in the stock market in early October of 1987 before the market crashed on October 19. What may have seemed to be a surefire good deal would have turned out to be not so good after all. While investments are a valid use for a home equity loan, you should follow the familiar advice of never investing more than you can afford to lose.

Consolidation loans are high risk also. Before you consider a home equity loan to consolidate all your other loans, think about what you're doing. If you're consolidating store and bank credit card charges where the payments are becoming unmanageable, either because each payment is too high or because there are too many different payments, and you think one payment at a lower level would be easier, you could be entering dangerous territory. In such a case, you have to look honestly at yourself and ask if your present situation developed because of poor credit or spending habits. If the answer is yes, you have to be sure you've cured yourself of those habits before putting a second mortgage on your home.

Actually, consolidation second mortgage loans are considered the highest risk of all the various loan purposes. The reason for this is that too many people take out the second mortgage thinking that more money is the answer to their problems when, in reality, it is the cause. What could happen is that you might become comfortable with your second mortgage payments once the stores and banks are no longer after you to make payments. So you consider using those credit cards again. If you go out on a shopping spree, you would again have store and bank card payments to make in addition to the second mortgage loan, and this time you can't get another second mortgage because you've borrowed all you can. Now, with a first mortgage loan, a second mortgage loan and additional credit card debt, the danger is very real that you will not be able to make all the payments. Being unable to repay a credit card debt can cause worry and a bad credit rating, but being unable to repay your equity loan can result in foreclosure and loss of your castle.

Pricing

After you've decided how much you need, you should carefully examine the pricing of the home equity loans that are available to you. There are several components of price. Most of these are discussed in detail in Chapter Six, including rate, APR and fees.

The price component that you'll notice first (and the one most heavily advertised) is the interest rate. This rate is expressed as an annual percentage rate or APR. The annual percentage rate is a true measure of the cost of your credit and is a yearly rate. It not only includes the interest on the loan but other charges as well, such as points or service charge. The Federal government requires that every lender provide the APR of a loan, so consumers can compare the true cost of credit.

Other considerations in pricing a home equity loan are up-front fees, such as application fees and points, all covered in more detail in Chapter Seven. Points are really just a service charge and are expressed as a percentage of the amount borrowed. For example, one point equals one percentage of the amount borrowed. On a $15,000 loan, one point is $150. Now here comes a quiz. Let's suppose you were offered the following two loans:

(1) $15,000 at ten percent for ten years with no up-front fees;
(2) $15,000 at 9.5 percent for 15 years, a fee of 1 point or $150, and an application fee of $165, for total up front fees of $315.

These two loans look very different, don't they? Well, in reality, if you kept both loans to maturity and included all up-front fees as part of the APR, they would equal the same APR of ten percent. The lower interest rate of 9.5 percent is raised to 10 percent by the additional $315 in fees. This is a good example of the tradeoff between points, fees and APR. However, this equality of pricing only works if you keep a loan to maturity or if you take the full ten years to pay off the loan. If you prepay the loan, then it's usually wiser to take a loan without points or up-front fees—a loan that isn't *loaded.* Using the same example again, the effective rate on loan (1) if prepaid in three years is still ten percent, whereas loan (2) if prepaid in three years has an effective rate of 10.36 percent.

When Should You Choose This Product?

When should you choose a closed end home equity loan over an open end loan or a line of credit? This is an excellent product to choose when you know you'll need a specific amount of money and you know that amount won't change. Purposes such as home improvement, bill consolidation, investment or education all work very well with a closed end home equity loan. For consumers who are nervous about taking out a second mortgage on their home but really need the funds for a large purchase or improvement, this is the product to select.

Advantages of a Closed End Loan

The main advantage of the closed end loan is that it is for a fixed amount, so you always know what your liability is; that liability is the amount you borrowed in the beginning. And because closed end loans can also be obtained at a fixed interest rate, there is the advantage of a known monthly payment, so this loan can be easily fit into your budget.

There is a high level of comfort in knowing what your monthly payment will be both today and a number of years from today. With a fixed rate loan you never have to worry about being caught off guard because of rising rates.

Another advantage of this product is that it is fully amortizing. Because it is closed end, you know that at the end of the term you will have fully paid off the loan. This is unlike the open end home equity line of credit or the balloon home equity loan that may result in not fully paying off the loan by the end of the term.

Disadvantages of a Closed End Loan

While there are numerous advantages to a closed end loan, there are also some disadvantages. You've seen the silver lining; here comes the gray cloud. For consumers who need different amounts of money from time to time, this may not be the correct loan. You may be better off with an open end loan where you can draw out as much as you need within your limits at one point in time, repay some and then draw it out again. If you are going to have the need for continually drawing out money, like a credit card, and you want to secure such a loan with the equity in your home, then a closed end loan is not the product for you. You would be better off looking at an open end home equity line of credit.

Also, if you are looking for some extremely short term financing, doing some repairs prior to selling your property, for example, a closed end loan may not be the loan for you. You would be better off with some other type of loan that allows more flexibility or at least a lower up-front fee structure.

Strategies

Although this loan is sometimes called the plain vanilla closed end loan, it probably doesn't seem quite so plain to you now, especially when you include the variable rate feature like caps and floors and indexing. This is a good product and has been around for many, many years. It is offered by most lenders and allows you both to take advantage of the equity in your property and to obtain some tax benefits that other types of consumer loans do not provide.

Now that you've read all the theory, what should you actually do? As experts who teach the bankers how to set up these loans, we have some definite opinions on what constitutes an advantageous closed end loan for a consumer.

First and foremost, your home is your castle, so don't risk it on frivolous purchases. If you feel uncomfortable with a second mortgage, stick with a closed end loan at a fixed rate. If the monthly payments of your fixed rate options are too expensive, lower the amount you plan to borrow. Maintaining the security of your home is the most important aspect, so budget wisely. Make sure you own the loan and that it doesn't own you.

You have a real choice between fixed rate or variable rate closed end loans, unlike open end loans where variable rate is all you will find. Both fixed and variable rate closed end loans are available. Which one you choose really depends on your needs. Variable rate is often priced lower, but fixed rate provides payment security. If you go with variable rate, know what the cap is and be sure you can afford the payments at the high end.

Your best choice for a cap is one that is not too high, and your best choice for a floor is none. More realistic is a cap allowing your rate to go up five percent or six percent and a floor allowing the rate to go down four percent or five percent. Your cap and floor should allow for almost the same change. Run, don't walk, away from any lender who offers a ten percent cap but only a two percent floor!

As an index, we suggest either prime or perhaps the T-bill rate. Prime has a slight advantage for you as a consumer in that it changes less frequently. Remember, however, that the spread is just as important. Based on historical rates, we would choose prime plus two percent rather than T-bill plus four percent. Stay away completely from an administered index or one where only the lender can determine when the rate will change.

You want your index to change weekly if rates are going down but yearly if rates are going up. But you're not going to be able to be that choosy. So, in general, the longer between rate changes, the better. Quarterly would be better than monthly.

Keep your term as short as possible, still with an affordable monthly payment. Don't let a lender talk you into a lower monthly payment without also knowing what it will cost you in additional interest.

The principal amount has more of an effect on your monthly payment than the rate does, so borrow only what you really need.

Any purpose is really acceptable provided you balance it against the fact that you are taking a second mortgage on your home. Just make sure the purpose is not frivolous, and be especially careful if you plan to use a home equity loan for investment or bill consolidation.

When considering fees, remember that up-front fees get more expensive if you prepay. The average first mortgage is paid off within seven years. If you don't plan to go to term with this loan, then shop for a lender offering lower front end fees.

Chapter Five

The Open End Home Equity Loan: *The New Product*

The open end home equity loan, or what is usually called the home equity line of credit, is the other major type of home equity loan. Some lenders have offered this type of loan for the past number of years, but it has really only become popular recently. It has now reached a peak of popularity and is currently the fastest growing type of equity loan on the market. In the financial industry it has attained the status of a superstar, and lenders proclaim this loan as both the consumer loan of the future and the product that will improve a depressed consumer lending market.

More people are asking about this type of loan than any other single type of equity loan. Consumer advocates, however, warn against this loan. The Consumers Union and The Consumer Federation of America both warn borrowers to be leery of this product and how it is used. Jane Bryant Quinn, the consumer columnist, calls this loan "poison."* The fact that this loan is so popular despite its hidden dangers only further points out its future potential.

How can a product be both so good and so bad at the same time? Well, it depends entirely on how it is used and how prudent you as the borrower are. Let's take a look at the open end home equity line of credit, what it is, how it works, and how you can use it best. We'll especially examine some of those pitfalls that the consumer advocates are talking about as well as some of the advantages that the lenders are pushing.

What Is an Open End Home Equity Loan?

Remember that a closed end home equity loan is like an automobile loan. You borrow a certain amount for a specified term or period of time,

* "What you should know about home equity loans," Jane Bryant Quinn, *Washington Post*, 10 August 1987.

and during that term you pay off the loan in equal amounts, month by month. An open end home equity loan is like a credit card. Instead of borrowing a set amount of cash up front, you get the right to receive any amount of cash you wish (up to your credit limit) at any time in the future. So instead of getting a check at the closing for the amount you want to borrow, you receive a credit line. Through this credit line you can at any point in time draw out any amount of the line that is available to you. For example, if your credit line were $25,000, you could draw out $5,000 today and $5,000 next week and keep drawing as much as you like until you reached the full $25,000 limit. And then as you repay and the amount outstanding drops to less than $25,000, you have the right to redraw up to the original limit of $25,000. So, just like a bank or department store credit card, you can constantly reuse the loan time after time, make some payments, redraw, and make some more payments. Basically, an equity line of credit is like a 20-pound credit card secured by a second mortgage on your house. Equity credit lines are very large and range from $10,000 to $500,000 or more and are usually based on both the equity in the real estate as well as the borrower's ability to repay the loan.

The basic features of an open end home equity line of credit, as opposed to a closed end home equity loan, are the following:

(1) The money is taken out over time depending on the needs of the borrower;

(2) Loan payment amounts under most plans will vary every period depending on the amount outstanding, although the percent due may be the same;

(3) At the end of the loan term, it is possible to have a large balance remaining, requiring a balloon payment or some other arrangement;

(4) Money can be borrowed at any time while the line of credit is available, usually through a convenient access device such as a checkbook.

Fixed Rate Versus Variable Rate

As with the closed end loan, the home equity line of credit can be found with either a fixed rate or a variable rate. However, you'll find most home equity lines of credit are at a variable rate.

Fixed Rate

The fixed rate home equity line of credit is offered by a very small percentage of the lenders in the marketplace, usually less than five percent.* There's a good reason why this is so; the following example will illustrate the potential problem, from a lender's point of view, with the fixed rate line.

Let's say you walk into your local lender and borrow $50,000 on an equity line of credit. You don't use any of the available credit line, so you leave the actual balance at zero. But you have an available line of $50,000 to be used any time between now and ten years from now. This loan is being offered to you at a fixed rate of 11.5 percent, which is probably .75 percent to 1 percent higher than a closed end home equity loan of the same term.

Now assume it is two years later, and interest rates have skyrocketed, repeating the scenario of 1980 and 1981 when prime rose from 11 percent up to 20.5 percent. Your lender, who also offers savings accounts, is offering a 30-month certificate of deposit at a rate of 17.5 percent. So, as a prudent financial consumer, you go to a teller and say, "Stella, let me have $50,000 from my credit line." You then take that $50,000 advance, for which you are paying 11.5 percent, and deposit it into a 30 month-CD at 17.5 percent. So without any effort on your part at all, you have just earned 6.5 percent on the lender's own money. While you will not win the Most Popular Customer of the Month Award from your lender, it is entirely legal to do this. The president may even send you a couple of free pens before he finds out where the deposit funds came from. It is for this reason that most lenders don't offer fixed rate lines of credit, because they're concerned about what may happen on future disbursements of the line if their savings rate ever exceeds the loan rate.

---

* Pricing $trategy Newsletter, November 1987, Moebs $ervices, Wadsworth, Illinois

A few lenders, however, are offering this product. This can only be for one of two possible reasons. One is that they really don't know what they're getting into and don't understand the product well enough. In this case they deserve to lose their money! The second is that they are smarter or larger than most other lenders and have the means to provide funds at a lower cost or to offset the possible interest rate risks through hedging or other money intestment techniques.

Variable Rate

The vast majority of open end home equity loans are variable rate, just as most closed end home equity loans are fixed rate. Unlike a closed end variable rate loan, the open end loan offers some protection or flexibility when the rate varies. Although a higher rate would apply to money you've already borrowed, you can choose not to borrow more if the rates go up. With a variable rate closed end loan, you've already borrowed the money, and if rates go up you simply have to pay it back at the higher rate. So if you're concerned about variable rates, you might want to consider open end home equity loans rather than closed end home equity loans for this reason.

Caps and Floors. As with variable rate closed end loans, variable rate open end loans will usually also have both caps and floors on the interest rate. A cap is the maximum percentage by which a rate can increase. And a floor is the maximum percentage by which a rate can decrease. Sometimes they're called rate ceilings and floors but never rate caps and shoes. Caps are for the protection of the consumer against unmanageably high interest rates, while floors are for the protection of the lender against unmanageably low interest rates.

When you shop for variable rate open end lines of credit, make sure to ask about caps and floors. Institutions are now required to have caps and to disclose those caps.

Caps and floors are discussed in detail in Chapter Seven.

Indexing. Variable rates are generally tied to an index, as was discussed in Chapter Four on closed end loans. An index is a base rate to which changes in your loan rate are tied. For example, your loan may be priced at three percent or four percent above prime, with the prime lending rate of banks being the index in this case. When that index changes, so does your rate. Common indexes are the prime rate, Treasury bill rate, Federal Home Loan Bank cost of funds rate, or an internal lender rate. Which rate is chosen should be of significant interest to you, and you should pay close attention when the lender explains the index to which your line of credit is tied. Some lending officers may not be familiar with the specifics of the index, but you should insist on having it explained to you. The choice of an index can have a significant impact on the cost of your loan. You'll usually receive a brochure about the index and a history of the rate changes

Another danger of variable rate lending connected with indexing is called negative amortization. This concept can be complicated, and it too can have a significant impact on the true cost of your loan.

Both indexes and negative amortization are covered in detail in Chapter Seven.

Frequency of Rate Change. Another variable rate feature is how often the rate changes. This could make a marked difference on the amount you pay in interest. In a rising rate environment, it would be to your best advantage to have your variable rate tied to an index that changes every quarter or every six months or even once a year, whereas if rates were going down you would want your loan rate to change every month.

There are two ways a variable rate can change.

The first option is for it to change at set periods. Lenders offer a variety of different programs with rate changes as often as monthly or as seldom as annually. If your index hasn't changed for three months, your rate won't change even if it's scheduled to change quarterly. And if the index then changes the day after the three months, your rate won't change for another quarter. Occasionally, you will find a program where the rate may change only every three years.

The other option is to change the rate when the index changes. Therefore, however long the index to which your rate is tied remains the same, your rate will stay the same. But when the index changes, then your rate changes, perhaps the next month. This works to your advantage if your loan uses a fairly stable index like prime but can be to your disadvantage if a volatile index like the Federal Home Loan Bank cost of funds is used.

How often your rate changes can be important. Open end loan rates tend to change more often than closed end rates, with the most common rate change frequency being monthly. Very rarely will you find a home equity line of credit which has a rate that changes only once a year.

Tiering

Tiering is a pricing structure that isn't found with closed end loans but does occur with lines of credit. Tiering is most familiar to consumers when associated with deposit products, such as money market deposit accounts, but it is not unusual to find it associated with lines of credit. On a deposit product, tiered accounts offer different interest rates depending on how high your balances are. With a loan product, tiering allows the lender to charge different rates for different outstanding balances. Normally, the higher the balance, the lower the rate, because it costs less on a relative basis for a lender to fund a big loan than a little loan.

There are two ways to tier. One way is called *progressive* and the other is *non-progressive*. These two types of tiering are illustrated in the examples that follow.

Example of Progressive Tiering

Using Table 5-1, assume that you have $40,000 outstanding on a $50,000 equity line of credit. The lender in this example has four tiers. On the first $10,000 of your loan, your rate is 11 percent. On the amount of money you borrowed between $10,001 and $15,000, your rate is 10.5 percent. On the amount you borrowed between $15,001 and $25,000, your rate is 10 percent. And on the rest, from $25,001 up to the $40,000 balance, the rate is 9.75 percent. So you are paying four different rates on your $40,000 outstanding. When the different rates are added together on a weighted average basis, your real interest rate is 10.22 percent. If you think this method is confusing, wait until you get your monthly statement. Your lender must provide full APR disclosures for each tier level.

Why do some lenders prefer progressive tiering? First, fewer and fewer do. But those that do offer this type of tiering do it so the institution

Table 5-1
Tiering Examples
Dollar Amount Outstanding = $40,000

Tier	*Rate*	*Progressive Tier Rate*	*Non-progressive Tier Rate*
$10,000 and under	11.00%	11.00% on first $10,000	-------
$10,001 - $15,000	10.50%	10.50% on next $ 5,000	-------
$15,001 - $25,000	10.00%	10.00% on next $10,000	-------
$25,001 and over	9.75%	9.75% on remainder	9.75% on all
Net rate you pay		10.22% blended rate	9.75% rate

can advertise a rate of 9.75 percent, their lowest rate even though in reality a particular loan may have a blended rate of 10.22 percent.

This type of tiering is very difficult to keep track of, and it can be impossible for consumers to calculate the interest rate if they use the credit line frequently.

Example of Non-Progressive Tiering

The other type of tiering is called non-progressive tiering. Again refer to Table 5-1. With this type of tiering, although the lender could have the same four tiers as with progressive tiering, you are charged only one interest rate, the one associated with your total outstanding balance. In the same example used above, if your balance were $8,000, then you would be charged 11 percent on your total loan. But if your balance were $22,000, then you would be charged an interest rate of ten percent on your entire loan balance.

Why do some lenders prefer non-progressive tiering? Institutions offer this type of tiering to encourage borrowers to maintain high balances, since the higher the balance, the lower the rate. Also, these lenders can still advertise the lowest rate.

It is important for you to know whether the lender you are considering has tiering and how it works. If you are planning to keep low outstanding balances, you may want to consider progressive tiering or no tiering. If, on the other hand, you plan to carry significant balances for some length of time and if the rate benefit is positive for you, you may prefer non-progressive tiering. Tiering can be very complicated, especially if you truly use the home equity line of credit like a credit card and the level of your balances fluctuates significantly.

Which Rate Type Should You Choose?

If you want a warm, secure feeling when you think about your loan, the best rate type you can choose is fixed rate. You have no risk of interest rate fluctuation with fixed rate. However, you will find that fixed rates are only offered for lines of credit at a premium price. Therefore, you would be paying a lot more for a fixed rate loan than you would for a variable rate loan. Unless you find someone who is having a sale on fixed rate equity lines of credit, you will generally be better off with the variable rate loans, because they will be offered at a much lower price.

If you plan on taking out the full amount immediately and keeping that amount outstanding for a long period of time, a fixed rate is for you. You then have the comfort of a known monthly payment. If, however, you plan to draw immediately only a portion of the loan and to hold the remainder of the line in reserve for future emergencies or anticipated expenses, you will probably want a variable rate loan because you can then choose when to borrow so as to take the loan within a lower interest-rate time frame.

Product Features

As you will see, the product features of this loan look much like the product features of a closed end loan. For both types of loans, you must consider term or maturity, the amount you want to borrow, the purpose for which you want to borrow, and the pricing you are offered on the loan. But in addition, you also need to consider something called an access device.

Term

When we discussed the term for a closed end loan, we saw that it was an important consideration because it directly affected the amount of the monthly payment. The longer the term, the lower the payment. This relationship does not hold, however, for open end home equity loans. For an open end loan, your term is usually stated as a maximum, and at the end of that maximum term, you may still have a balance remaining on your loan, so the balance and the term do not have the same relationship in open end credit as they do in closed end credit. Therefore, as with a credit card, there will be instances where you will pay more than the minimum payment just to reduce the balance to either open up more available credit or to reduce interest payments.

With a home equity line of credit, you can't assume that it will fully amortize, or that it will be fully paid off at the end of the term. The very nature of this loan allows you at the end of the term, which could be anywhere from five to fifteen years, to still have the full amount of the loan outstanding. In other words, two days before the maturity date you could draw money up to your maximum available line of credit and, unless you had a way of repaying it within two days, when the loan "matured" you would still owe the full balance on the loan.

This characteristic can be both an advantage and a disadvantage. It can work to the favor of consumers who repay loans in large sums, such as those who are using the loans to fund investments. However, if you plan to borrow the full amount a year before the term runs out—for a car purchase, for example—and then you only pay the minimum payment every month, having a large sum due at the end of the term can be a disaster. And what is your answer to a lender who says, "Your loan is now expired; please pay us $40,000?" You would do well to plan for this contingency.

Principal Amount

The amount borrowed with a home equity line of credit will probably be different than under a closed end loan. A closed end loan is generally used for a specific purpose and is therefore for a predetermined amount. A loan sufficient to serve that purpose is generally all a consumer would want to borrow, even if more equity were available in the property and a bigger loan could be obtained. With an equity line of credit, however, the consumer often has no specific purpose in mind. You may need $8,000 now for home improvement, but you don't know what you may need in the future. So you will generally take out an equity line for most of the equity in your house, even though you have no current intention of using the whole line. Because of this, the equity pledged generally tends to be higher on this type of loan.

There is some danger in this. It's nice to be able to get a large line of credit to use as you please, but you have to be honest with yourself as to whether you can handle that amount of credit. If you tend to use however much credit you're given, then this is not the loan for you; the worst thing that could happen is to spend that available credit on luxuries or frivolous items. It has happened that people have nickeled and dimed away the entire equity in their homes. This is another reason consumer advocates caution against this loan. The old adage applies here—consumer beware!

Purpose

Possible purposes for which home equity lines of credit are used are fairly similar to those for which closed end home equity loans are used. Common purposes (in the order of preference*) are home improvement, business or investments, bill consolidation, purchase of an auto or truck, or education. These purposes were described in Chapter Four but are reviewed briefly here.

The single most popular use is for home improvement, especially where multiple payouts are required. You could borrow the whole amount needed for the home improvement up-front, but then you would be paying interest on the full loan whereas you may only need a portion of the money at a time. And remember that few home improvements will give you a dollar-for-dollar return in the housing market, so make sure the improvement has personal value for you.

Educational expenses are often funded by home equity lines of credit. The payouts required for education are very similar to the multiple payouts required for home improvement, except that there is

---

* *Home Equity Loans II*, Market Facts, Inc., Chicago, and Moebs $ervices, Wadsworth, Illinois.

more time between payouts. Most school expenses are paid on a quarter or semester basis, which is a great match to the flexibility of a line of credit. In this way, you only pay interest on the amount you need at the time.

Funding investments with home equity lines of credit is risky but perhaps not as risky as funding them with a fixed rate closed end home equity loan. The nature of investments often requires some flexibility, and a line of credit is more suited to this purpose than a fixed loan would be. The major caution here, of course, is to never invest more money than you can afford to lose, especially if you're borrowing on your home to make some surefire investment.

Finally, bill consolidation as a use for home equity line of credit money is quite risky, as was discussed in Chapter Four. If you've gotten yourself in trouble with your other lines of credit, a home equity line of credit isn't going to solve your problems.

This product is particularly well-suited for a small business loan. Normally, a small business owner who needs a business loan would apply in the commercial loan department of a bank to borrow money. Since he is not the Chairman of General Motors, the owner is not going to get a loan at prime rate; so small business loans are usually quite expensive. Also, in order to secure a small business loan the lender takes the rights to not only all the business assets but usually also to the personal assets, including the home.

Many business owners have realized it is just as easy to make a right turn into the consumer loan department to get an equity line of credit instead of a left turn into the business loan department. The equity line works about the same as a business loan in that it is a revolving line of credit. But it is often less expensive than the business loan since it's considered to be less risky. After all, a small business loan relies primarily on the business assets, although the home may serve as secondary collateral, but an equity loan relies primarily on the home for security. So business investment is becoming the number two purpose for a home equity line of credit.

Another use for the home equity line of credit is to replace the traditional auto or general purpose consumer loan. The equity line has been called the ultimate consumer loan of the future when used in the following way. Based on the equity in your home, you open an equity line of credit. You don't use the loan immediately but keep it in reserve as a replacement for other types of consumer loans that you currently have. Eight months after you open up your equity line of credit, you decide it is the time to buy another car. You walk into the dealer's showroom, you find the car you want, and when you're ready to close the sale you pull out your equity line checkbook and write a check for the car. GMAC can jump in the lake, unless, of course, it's a GMAC equity line.

The reason this is especially attractive is that your alternative is to apply for a conventional auto loan. This can take time to get approved and delay the delivery of the car. And you would have to leave the auto title as security with the lender. In addition, under the new tax law, interest on an auto loan is no longer fully deductible when you itemize your taxes.

On the other hand, if you write an equity line check, you can immediately drive out with the car and the title in your back pocket. Interest is most likely fully deductible on your itemized tax return, and your equity line rate is probably less than automobile loan rates. You could then structure the repayment of this auto loan any way you want, assuming the payments you make are at least the minimum required under your line. If your equity line has a ten-year maximum, then you can pay off your auto loan in five years and do this all over again for another five years with another new car.

Keep in mind, however, that if you only make minimum payments rather than treating this like a regular auto loan to be repaid in 48 months and thus wind up stretching out the payments over the full ten or 15 years, the extra interest you pay and the up-front fees that were paid at closing would probably have made a conventional auto loan cheaper.

Pricing

Most of the components of pricing, such as rate, APR, and fees, are discussed in Chapter Seven. However, some aspects of pricing are peculiar to an open end line of credit.

Markets are very competitive for home equity lines of credit, and it is possible to get this type of loan without spending too much money in up-front fees. However, beware of all the hidden costs that can accompany a line of credit. A loan with a lot of these fees is called *loaded* while one that has few fees is called a *no load* loan. While the interest rate of the loan will probably be fairly uniform within your market, fees can vary tremendously.

If, for example, you had a one percent up-front fee on a home equity open end loan, this would not be one percent of the amount you actually borrowed but rather one percent of the total line. So even if you borrow only $10,000 of your $30,000 line of credit, if the up-front fee is one percent, your fee would be one percent of $30,000 or $300.

Other fees include an application fee, paid at time of application, an annual fee, a closing fee, and points. Like many types of loans, home equity lines of credit often charge application fees. And just like credit cards, many home equity lines charge an annual fee. A closing fee is charged to pay for the process of closing and document preparation. Points are basically a service fee to pay for the processing of the loan. All the fees mentioned here, plus some additional ones, are discussed in detail in Chapter Seven.

Because of the highly competitive nature of this product, it is more likely that you will be able to find a no load equity line product offered by one of your local lenders. In this case, your only fees would be closing costs such as appraisal and title fees, but fees such as application fees and points would be waived. There are some real bargains around with the open end loan, so check with more than one lender before you decide on whom to use.

Access Devices

With an equity line, unlike a closed end loan, you don't receive all your cash at one time at the closing. You receive it over time. So you must have a way to draw out the money when you need it. These ways are called *access devices,* and they are unique to open end lines of credit. Access devices are discussed in detail in Chapter Six.

One way to draw money on your line of credit is by an in-person draw at the financial institution. You physically go to the lender, fill out a form, and request the money in person.

Another method is a check access. You receive a checkbook at the closing and write a check just as if this were your checking account. With check access, there is often a minimum amount for which you can write a check, such as for at least $500.

The third access device, often used in conjunction with a check access, is a credit card. You are issued either a Visa or a MasterCard, and you can then access your equity line from that credit card. We suggest you avoid credit card access as it adds very little utility to the loan and makes it too easy to nickel and dime away your home equity. Other forms of access are almost as convenient and would give you more protection. However, if owning a $30,000 credit card is one of your life's goals, then go for it!

When Should You Choose This Product?

You can best use this product if you have multiple needs to tap your equity over a period of time. An example of this would be a major home improvement which requires multiple payouts. If you were having a room addition constructed, you would normally pay the contractor a down payment amount upon signing the contract. Then, when the materials are delivered you usually make a second payment. After a certain percentage of the work is completed you would make another payment, and upon completion you would pay the final amount. This process could take a number of months depending upon how complicated the home improvement is. If you had taken out the traditional closed end loan, you would have borrowed the full cost of the improvement and would have had to pay interest to the lender on this total amount even though you were not using all of it yet. With an equity line of credit, you would only pay interest on the amount that you draw and would therefore only pay interest when you were actually using the funds.

This type of use is why the home equity line of credit is considered by many to be the consumer loan of the future under the new tax rules. You would now no longer have to go through a tiresome application process every time you want to borrow for a consumer purchase.

Advantages of an Open End Loan

The primary advantage of the open end loan clearly is the availability of money when you need it without having to pay interest until the funds are drawn down. It can be used as a cash reserve just sitting there waiting to be used when required. If you need a large amount of money which you could turn over rapidly, then consider using an open end loan. An ideal use would be for an investment or other business use. You could also use a home equity line of credit for expenses where the actual cash paid out would vary over time, like a home improvement or educational expenses. Or, if you are able to budget yourself carefully, you could use this loan to buy a car or other consumer type good.

Disadvantages of an Open End Loan

There are, however, some serious disadvantages to this loan. First, a specific danger, mentioned by consumer advocates, is that there could be a very high cap on this loan that would allow your payments to go higher than you may be able to manage. While lenders must now tell you what the cap is, there is no limit on lenders other than their state laws to control how high a cap can go, so theoretically a lender could have a cap of 50 percent. That's unlikely because, of course, competition would kill them, but this danger should be kept in mind.

But the primary danger of this loan is the significant responsibility that rests with the person borrowing the money—you! This is a disadvantage about which consumer groups are very concerned, and about which they repeatedly warn. Be honest with yourself as to whether you are the type of person who can maturely handle a lot of credit. If you're likely to use up the credit line on frivolous purchases just because the money is available, you may end up squandering all the equity in your home with nothing to show for it. And if you plan to use this loan for bill consolidation because other credit products were abused, an equity line won't solve your problem. Finally, if you don't manage the loan wisely, you may end up owing $40,000 when the loan matures, and where are you going to come up with $40,000 tomorrow to pay this loan off? So, if you tend to abuse credit or have trouble handling credit and you think you may want to try to use this product to solve all your problems, getting an equity line would be like swapping deck chairs on the Titanic. There may be some temporary improvement, but the end result will be the same.

Strategies

Your choice as to whether to go with a fixed or a variable rate for your open end line of credit is really made for you. Fixed rates on open end credit are, for the most part, only available from the large national lenders rather than the smaller local lenders, and it's a sure bet that you will have to accept a variable rate.

A cap that is not too high and no floor is your best choice. More realistic is a cap allowing your rate to go up five percent to six percent and a floor allowing the rate to go down four percent to five percent. Your cap and floor should be approximately equivalent. Avoid any lender who offers a ten percent cap but only a two percent floor!

As an index, we suggest either prime or the T-bill rate. Prime has a slight advantage in that it changes less frequently. Remember, however, that spread is just as important. Based on historical rates, we would choose prime plus two percent rather than T-bill plus four percent. Stay away completely from an administered index.

You want your index to change weekly if rates are going down but yearly if rates are going up. But you won't be able to find this perfect index! So, in general, the longer between rate changes the better.

Our experience with tiering is that it's more complicated to understand and more trouble to track than it's worth. We advise against it.

As to the length of term that is best, with an open end loan, the end of the term means any balance remaining is due in full. If that makes you uncomfortable, ask your lender what provisions there are at the end of the term. Some lenders provide for a renewal or roll any balance into a closed end amortizing loan.

Our final comment is to repeat that this loan is not for everyone. Know yourself and your spending habits before you take out a home equity line of credit. If you find you really need the flexiblity of an open end loan but are concerned about tempting yourself with using too much of your equity, look for a lender who uses the in-office draw for an access device. When you must go into your lender's office to take out the money, you find this process is self-regulating and removes the temptation for all but the greatest needs. Also, we strongly encourage you to read the following chapter to understand some of the day-to-day issues encountered with home equity lines of credit.

This is a great product and truly can become *the* consumer loan of the future. And what's even better, due to competition this loan is on sale; compared to other products it's relatively cheap.

Chapter Six

Day-to-Day Issues for Home Equity Lines of Credit

Your loan has been approved, you have signed all the papers, so now what? A lot of things, that's what. Let's take a look at what happens on a daily basis after you've got the loan. These day-to-day issues are of concern primarily for the equity line of credit. The line of credit has more day-to-day transaction capability, and consumers usually have more transactions with it than with a regular closed end second mortgage. With the closed end second mortgage, you receive your money, you go out and spend it, and then you make your monthly payments. At least lenders hope you do. That's all there is to it. But with the equity line of credit, funds are coming in as payments, funds are going out as draws, and the number of transactions on the account, which approximates a credit card in its nature, can be quite high. It is worthwhile to discuss some of the unique servicing problems connected with equity lines of credit, which is what this chapter is all about.

When Can You Draw Funds?

You just walked out of the loan closing, and now you have two important questions—when can you draw funds from your equity line and how much can you draw? When you can draw funds is restricted by when you signed your right of rescission. Chapter Eleven covers this document which assures that there is a "cooling-off" period of three days required by law just in case you should change your mind. You may not draw any funds during those three business days. After those three days, you will be required to sign a confirmation of the right of rescission stating that you're not rejecting the loan. You can then draw as much of the funds as you wish up to the credit limit established by your lender.

How Much Can You Draw?

The amount you can draw is governed by two parameters—how much and how little. How much is limited by the maximum amount of your credit line. How little may also be restricted by the policies of your lender. Some lenders have no minimum, so you could draw as little as you want, even $1. But a number of lenders have put a lower limit or a floor on the amount that you can draw from your equity line, usually between $500 and $1,500. The purpose of this limitation is so that you don't use the equity in your home for minor purchases. It should be understood by all parties that this loan is meant for major purchases and should be used that way.

A restriction on the minimum withdrawal can be circumvented by writing a check for the minimum amount, buying the minor item, and then repaying the rest. And if you repay the same day, you probably won't even be charged interest. This entire transaction can take place right at the teller window. However, this is a bit of a hassle. And doing this too many times may result in a chat between you and your lender. A number of lenders have a stipulation somewhere in the agreement that you signed that prohibits this sort of thing.

Access Devices—a Convenience and a Danger

Since you don't get all your money up front with this account, as you would with a closed end loan, you need some means to get your money over time. These means are called *access devices* and can be one of three types. The first type is the *draw,* where you must physically go into the financial institution and fill out a voucher to request a draw against your account. The second type is *check access,* where you receive a separate checkbook that allows you to write checks against your line. And the third type is a *credit card,* which allows you electronic access into your equity line account.

While these three types of access devices all achieve the same purpose, which is to allow you to draw funds, each has a level of danger in addition to a level of convenience. And the two go hand in hand: the higher the level of convenience, the higher the level of danger. We define danger here as your ability to spend the equity in your home on minor items or purchases. Most people who take out this loan are fiscally responsible and will probably spend their equity money in a prudent manner. Let's also be realistic. Some people, if offered the easiest access (the credit card type of access), will end up frittering away the equity line. As stated earlier, the equity line of credit is not a loan for everyone, and it is hoped that a screening process took place during credit approval. But a lender can't be responsible for how well this account will be used in all cases. A major part of that responsibility rests on someone else's shoulders—yours.

The In-office Draw

The in-office draw is the most conservative of the three types of access and makes it the most difficult to draw funds. Any time you want money you must physically go into the lending institution and make a formal request by filling out a form or a request voucher. The lender will then issue you either a check or cash. While this is not very convenient, that very inconvenience gives you protection against yourself. You probably would not personally request funds unless it were for a good purpose. Of course, there's the convenience factor. Besides, if the amount requested is large you may need to get officer approval, and when you're face to face with the officer who's going to authorize release of your funds there's always the fear that you may be refused. Although that's highly unlikely, it can happen. So usually a customer will only go in with a good reason for the draw. This form of access protects you from casual use of your home's equity and prohibits you from spending it on frivolous items.

In-office access also protects you against the fraudulent use of your account by anyone else. It's unlikely that anyone other than a legitimate borrower will go in and physically request a draw.

Not all lenders offer in-person draws, so check with the institution you're considering. If you feel you might be the type who would spend your home's equity on unnecessary items, you may want to consider this method of access to your credit line.

Check Access

The most common access type is the check. You receive a checkbook with a certain number of checks, and when you want money you write a check just as if it were a regular checking account. There may be a minimum amount for the check that you can write, and it may be printed right on the face of the check that it is not valid for less than $500 or $1,000. Check access is more popular than in-person draws, because it is much more convenient and allows you more freedom while still maintaining some degree of security.

Check access has a little higher risk than the in-office draw as far as the lender is concerned, but it provides a greater level of customer convenience. This is why check access is the most common; it straddles the middle ground between convenience for the user and risk for the lender. However, although the minimum amount does protect you from the frivolous use of the funds to some degree, fiscal maturity is still needed when you have checkbook access to your home's equity.

Fraud risk is a little higher on a check-accessed account than an in-office draw. If you must physically visit the financial institution to get any money from your account (unless someone impersonates you), only *you* have access to the account. It's possible, however, for you to lose your checkbook or have it stolen. That's bad enough when it's a normal checking account where the thief may have access to perhaps $500. But it can be really brutal if you have $50,000 in available credit. What is even more difficult is when not only the checkbook is missing but also a wallet containing photo IDs, such as a driver's license. This is the perfect entree for the crook to go out on a shopping spree. So it becomes very important for you to safeguard your checkbook at all times. If you lose the checkbook, immediately report it to your lender, so a stop can be placed on all checks and new ones issued. It is ultimately the lender that would have to suffer any loss if fraud were to occur, but it's still not a pleasant situation. Besides, why should the thief who stole from you travel to Hawaii if you can't?

Credit Card Access

Credit card access has the highest level of convenience and accessability. Usually, you will not find a lender that offers credit card access alone; this type of access is usually offered in conjunction with one of the other two methods, such as checking.

This access device can be very dangerous. It's easy to nickel and dime your home's equity away for small purchases with a credit card. Most consumers use a credit card for convenience for small purchases so that they don't have to carry a lot of cash around. Therefore, credit card purchases tend to be between $10 and $500. To now use this equity line credit card for only large purchases means you need to change the way you're accustomed to using a credit card. Otherwise, you can easily use this line for clothing purchases or even food purchases. We advise strongly against using your home's equity for consumables. Having a beer at the local bistro is not a good use of your home's equity.

From the lender's point of view, credit card access should only be given to the most prudent borrowers. A credit card increases the likelihood that the user of this account will draw on the real estate's equity frequently for small amounts. It is almost impossible to place a minimum limit on the amount of a purchase on a credit card, so credit card access can be used for just about any small purchase. Credit card access is not particularly popular and is only used by ten percent or fewer of the lenders across the country.

From the standpoint of fraud, having a credit card with an eligible line that equals the equity in your home is very dangerous. Actually, the danger is not so much to you, since you are still protected under the same credit card rule that applies to a Visa card or MasterCard. But the danger of fraud is very high for the lender. Although you may be liable only for the first $50 of any fraudulent purchase, the lender is liable for the remainder. When a credit card has a line of $50,000 or more, lenders can get a bit nervous. Using credit cards fraudulently is fairly easy for a professional. If you lose a credit card connected to your equity account, notify your lender immediately, so they can take the proper steps to restrict the use of the lost card and reissue you a new card.

Access to an equity line with a credit card should only be used by consumers who are fiscally responsible and have some need for credit card access to large amounts of cash. For most of us, credit card access is really unnecessary. Even though it may be fun to be able charge a car, it's really just as easy to write a check, and this is the access device we recommend.

The Billing Statement—
Your Window on Your Loan Transactions

One of the best ways to comprehend what's happening to your loan on an ongoing basis is to understand your billing statement. The rules a lender must follow for reporting the transactions on your equity line account in the billing statement are basically the same rules that credit card companies must follow for their billing statement. These rules are required by the same federal laws.

The purpose of your monthly billing statement is to provide you with a record of the activity on your account during the cycle, indicate the cost of your credit, and request payment if any is due. You will normally find the following information, as is required by Federal law, in your billing statement:

1. Identification of the lender.
2. The amount of any previous balance.
3. Any draws on your account during the billing period or any charges if you use a credit card during the billing period.
4. Identification of transactions.
5. Your APR and your periodic rates.
6. Balance on which the finance charge was assessed.
7. The amount of the finance charge.
8. Any other charges, such as an annual fee if assessed and credit insurance charges.
9. Closing date of your billing cycle.
10. Opening date of your billing cycle.
11. The number of days in the billing cycle.
12. The new balance.
13. The payment due.
14. Your billing rights information.

There are other items that are not required by Federal law that you will probably see in most billing statement. They include:

1. Customer service phone number.
2. Your available credit.
3. Any delinquent amount.
4. Your account number.

5. Your return-payment coupon allowing you to make payment through the mail.

It is important that you monitor this billing statement closely, because it provides you with all the information on your account on a month-to-month basis. If anything happens to mess up the account, this is where you will catch it.

Your Billing Rights

As stated earlier, you have the same rights on an equity line account that you do with a credit card, including any billing disputes. Because this account is a revolving line of credit, you have all the rights of the provisions within the Fair Credit Billing Act. Under this Federal legislation, the billing rights work as follows:

1. Within 60 days after receiving a statement, you may question any transactions, whether a debit or a credit to the account, appearing on a statement. You must place this dispute in writing; telephone calls do not protect you under the law. Also, you must have this dispute placed in writing and sent to the lender within the 60-day period, or your rights on the disputed item will expire.
2. Your lender is then required to acknowledge receipt of the billing dispute within 30 days of actual receipt unless they immediately correct the error prior to the end of that 30 days.
3. Within 90 days, the lender must either correct the error or explain to you why the bill is correct.
4. Once your lender receives your initial letter claiming a dispute, they cannot collect from you the disputed amount, collect from you any interest on the disputed amount, calculate a monthly payment based on a balance with the disputed amount as part of the balance, or report the disputed amount as delinquent while it is in dispute.
5. If the disputed amount is the lender's error, all the interest on the disputed amount must be waived.
6. If the disputed amount was not the lender's error but was a valid posting and/or it was your error, then you are responsible for the principal amount as well as any accrued interest. The lender

must first, however, notify you in writing of the specific amounts that you owe.

7. During the dispute period you cannot withhold payments on any undisputed amounts or undisputed balances; you must continue payments on all other amounts not in dispute.

These rights must be disclosed to you in your initial agreement and many times they will also be found printed in your monthly credit card statement. At a minimum, they must be sent to you bi-annually.

Billing Disputes with Credit Card Access

One other thing you should remember if you have a credit card access equity line is that this line of credit still falls under the special rules for credit card purchases.

If you have a problem with the quality of goods or services that you purchased with a credit card and you have tried in good faith to correct the problem with the merchant, you may have another avenue of action against the merchant. You have this protection only if the purchase price is more than $50 and the purchase was made in your home state or within 100 miles of your mailing address. However, if the lender owns or operates the merchant or if the lender mailed you an advertisement for the property or service that you purchased with the credit card, then all purchases are covered regardless of the amount or location of the purchase. The procedure to follow is the same as is used with a billing dispute. You would write to the lender that you dispute a credit card purchase or that you made a credit card purchase and did not get the service you required or that you returned the product. The merchant then has the right to answer that dispute. What goes on from there could range from something very simple to a long series of negotiations.

Other Servicing Issues

From time to time other servicing issues may arise regarding this product. It's worthwhile to examine two of these issues up front as to what the lender's position will be.

Credit Line Increase Requests

Don't expect a lender to allow any increase in your credit line. Unlike a bankcard, this is an equity line of credit secured by a second mortgage. If the lender were to increase your credit line, they must also change the filing of the second mortgage and the recording of the collateral instrument. Because this is a very cumbersome procedure and requires a new appraisal, new title search,and other costs, it is normally not worth the lender's time nor is it worth the expense to you. If you are asking for a significant increase, then you will most likely be required to close this loan and request a new loan—in other words, to refinance.

Substitution Of Collateral

With many types of consumer loans, such as an automobile loan or a collateralized personal loan, lenders may allow borrowers to substitute collateral. For example, a lender may have title to a particular car for collateral, but then the borrower wants to substitute another car so the first one can be sold. Lenders often allow this as an accommodation to their customers. With an equity line of credit, however, this cannot be allowed because of the mortgage filing and recording. To substitute collateral would require refiling an entirely new mortgage as well as doing a new appraisal, new title search, and so forth. What lenders will normally do is state that if you wish to substitute collateral, you must close one loan and apply for a new loan. This, of course, will result in all new fees for you to pay, but you may be able to negotiate some of them with your lender.

Strategies

Using and monitoring your equity line of credit is fairly simple, but there are some common sense rules that need to be followed. Part of that common sense involves simply understanding what's involved. You can then protect yourself and your lender, and both of you will benefit.

Our general advice is to stay away from credit card access. It really is more than you need. Check access is our favorite because it hits the happy medium between protecting you from yourself and giving you the convenience you need and want.

For the equity line of credit, your billing statement truly is your window to what is happening on your account. Pay close attention to it each month, and be sure you agree with it or contact your lender right away.

Chapter Seven

Cost of a Home Equity Loan: *Rate, APR, Fees*

You better pay attention when you read this chapter. Pricing of home equity loans can be fun, but it is also complicated. Features that initially appear to be favorable can upon closer examination turn out to be not at all favorable. As experts, we will be with you to guide you through the maze of the costs of home equity loans. Let's start with APR.

APR

When it comes time to add up the costs of your equity loan, the single most expensive item is interest. That's why it is important to understand interest rates.

Prior to 1969, lenders were allowed to advertise and disclose rates almost any way they wanted. It was possible for a lender to advertise an interest rate of nine percent when the true cost would be closer to 16 percent. To stop abuses of this kind, Congress in 1969 enacted Truth in Lending legislation, commonly called Regulation Z by lenders. Reg Z stated that while a lender could still calculate the interest rate in the old way, another rate would also have to be disclosed—the Annual Percentage Rate (APR). The APR would include certain fees considered by Congress to be part of the cost of credit, such as points and, under some conditions, application fees. Not all fees would be included; excluded for real estate secured loans are those that would vary with the individual loan such as appraisal costs, title costs, or costs of credit checks. The purpose of the APR disclosure was and is to provide one uniform method of calculating the cost of credit, thus allowing consumers to comparison shop. Now all lenders must include the APR when advertising or disclosing credit terms.

By looking at the APR, it is possible to identify that two lenders with identical rates really have different costs of credit. An example is shown below:

	Lender A	*Lender B*
Interest rate	12.00%	12.00%
Other fees	None	.25%
APR	12.00%	12.25%

Lender A has no other "costs of credit," such as a service charge, so the rate and the APR are the same. Lender B has a service charge, the effect of which is to increase your true cost of credit, the APR, to 12.25 percent.

When shopping for a loan, you need to get the APR as well as the rate. Rates can be misleading when comparing the costs of loans from two different lenders. You're better off using the APR. Only keep in mind that even the APR doesn't include all the different costs that can vary from lender to lender. But it's a good place to start.

Enter Freddie, Fannie, and Ginnie

No discussion on pricing or fees of loans is complete without introducing you to Freddie, Fannie and Ginnie. While these may sound like a threesome looking for a fourth for bridge, they really are key players in the secondary market. And these three have a major influence on the pricing and product features of home equity loans.

The primary market can be described thus: you go to a lender for a loan, sign the paperwork, the lender gives you money, and the lender keeps the loan until it's paid off by you. In the secondary market, everything is the same from your perspective except that the lender sells your loan to a third party. This third party can be another lender but more often is Freddie Mac (Federal Home Loan Mortgage Corporation), Fannie Mae (Federal National Mortgage Association) and Ginnie Mae (Government National Mortgage Association).

Why do lenders sell your loan? Basically for liquidity reasons. They can take the money they get from selling your loan and make a new loan. The lender normally continues to service your loan (i.e., collect your payments and send you statements), so you probably wouldn't even know that it's sold. And it wouldn't make any difference to you if you did know.

When your lender sells a loan to the secondary market, the buyers, such as Fannie Mae or Freddie Mac, pay your lender the amount of the loan. For example, your lender would sell a $100,000 loan for $100,000 (provided the loan rate matches the institutional buyer's required yield). The institutional buyer, of course, gets to collect the interest. In order for a loan to be saleable in the secondary market, it must meet certain structure and profit requirements. The loan must have a certain yield. If the interest rate is not high enough to interest the institutional buyer, the lender may also offer the institutional buyer part of the points or application fees.

This is a very long way around to get to the point of this discussion of the secondary market. If the loan is to be sold in the secondary market, and if the interest rate is also to be low enough to be competitive to potential consumers, then loan fees must be added to the loan in order to make its yield attractive to potential purchasers in the secondary market.

Now, if the loan is sold in the secondary market, the lender has made their profit up front through the types of fees described here. In addition, they recover the principal immediately by selling the loan. They can then turn around and relend the $100,000 for more up-front fees to someone else. The lender may or may not retain the month-to-month servicing of the loan. If they do service the loan for the new institutional owner, which is the usual case, they would also earn money by charging a servicing fee.

Lines of credit, on the other hand, do not have an active secondary market. Like a credit card, there is no set amortization period. A loan could be paid down by half and then redrawn for the full amount. Since open end credit provides for uneven cash flow, the desire to purchase by an institutional buyer from the secondary market for this type of credit is limited. So lenders typically keep these loans in the portfolio, meaning that they do not sell them. Because of this, they are less concerned with the fees and getting all their profit up front and are willing to look at the loan as a long-term proposition and collect their profits down the road through the collection of interest.

Up-Front Fees

Want to save hundreds of dollars? Then pay close attention to up-front fees. The understanding of up-front fees is critical in your selection of a home equity loan because these types of fees can have a major impact on the true cost of your loan. Also, lenders will often not explain them as well as they might.

Loan Fee Grouping

We said that this loan can be confusing. And one of the confusing things about one-time fees connected with home equity loans is that lenders may group them in different ways. Title fees, for example, could be part of points or part of closing costs. Most groups of fees can be broken down into three basic fee types as follows: application fees, points and closing costs. The points must be included in the APR as a cost of credit, but application fees and closing costs are not required to be included in the APR. So how much a loan appears to cost can be greatly influenced by where lenders make their profit. An aggressive lender may advertise a low APR with no points in order to appear to be competitive. But they're actually making their profit in high closing costs. So, in reality, you end up paying more in total than you would with a competing lender that groups closing costs into the points and discloses them as part of the APR, which as a result appears higher.

Because of the grouping possibility, you need to look at more than just APR. You also need to analyze the three major fee groups, which are described later in this chapter.

Fees for Open End Versus Closed End Loans

A basic difference between the closed end loan and the open end line of credit is that you're much more likely to encounter fees with a closed end loan than a line of credit. The closed end loan, you may recall, is similar to an auto loan. A fixed amount is lent for a fixed term, and it is normally fully paid off by the time the maturity is reached. Fees with this type of loan would include an application fee, points, and closing costs. The line of credit product is similar to a credit card, and the fees are often less for this product.

There are two reasons why fees are more common for closed end loans than for lines of credit. One is competition. Competition is heavier for the line of credit since this is the newer of the two types of home equity loans. Lenders may thus offer lines of credit to their home equity loan applicants as "specials." This is a real plus for you since these lenders, in their desire to make more loans and gain greater market share, advertise their product on a price basis. They will cut the price or the up-front fees in order to try and bring in more business. It is quite expensive to initially establish a loan or a credit line, and it is quite possible for a lender in a competitive environment who decides not to charge any up-front costs to make little or no money on the loan. On the other hand, you can benefit from this.

A second reason fees may be less for a line of credit compared to a a closed end loan is because of the secondary market. Lenders can sell standard closed end second mortgage loans that they have originated to the secondary market, which, as discussed earlier, requires fees.

Application Fee

If the lender charges an application fee, it normally covers the cost of processing the application. It can include some costs that are usually considered to be closing costs, such as the appraisal or title, and it can also include the credit check fee. Some institutions don't have an application fee. They include the costs of processing in the closing fees. So if the loan doesn't close, there is no cost to you. The application fee is normally collected at the time the application is accepted and can range from $25 to $300.

Know what you're getting into, and ask the lenders whether their application fee is refundable. In other words, if the loan does not close, do you get any or all of the application fee back? An application fee can be one of three types:

(1) It may not be refundable no matter what the circumstances.

(2) It may be refundable if the lender turns you down but not if you turn the lender down—that is, if the lender refuses to make the loan for any reason, whether for credit problems or because the loan doesn't meet their standards, you get the application fee back. However, if the lender is willing to make the loan and you change your mind, then they keep the fee.

(3) Finally, the entire application fee may be refundable if the loan doesn't close for any reason.

Many institutions do not have an application fee for a home equity loan, but if you are considering one that does, be sure you understand the institution's refund policy. In general, the application fee is more common with closed end loans than for open end credit lines, so if you're applying for a closed end loan, you're more likely to run into application fees.

Points

Points are also called a service charge. You probably ran into these once before, when you purchased your house. They are very common on first mortgage loans. Points are calculated as a percentage of the loan amount for a closed end loan or the amount of line granted for an open end line of credit. One point equals one percent. For example, if you applied for a $30,000 closed end loan or a $30,000 equity line of credit, if the lender charged you one point, that would be $300. Points are normally collected at the closing and not at time of application.

Closing Costs

Closing costs cover a variety of different items, and, in fact, closing costs may be the single largest up-front cost to you in obtaining your loan. They include appraisal fees, title fees, recording fees, attorney's fees, closing fees if a third-party closing agent is used, and document preparation fees. Not all lenders charge for all items, and some lenders may include them in the points or the application fee. Some lenders will absorb these costs themselves, so you don't have to pay for them at all.

Appraisal Fees. Appraisals cost about $144, based on the type of appraisal as well as the type of property. Appraisals on commercial and business real estate cost more than appraisals on residential real estate, but $144 is the average for a residential appraisal.* The various types of appraisals will be covered in detail in Chapter Nine. Note that $144 is the national average, but your costs may vary considerably depending on your market conditions.

* Pricing $trategy Newsletter, Moebs $ervices, August, 1987.

Title Fees. The title fee, also called title search, is the fee for researching the title or lien history on your property. It verifies for the lender that you really own the property, and if there are any challenges to that ownership, such as tax liens, mechanics' liens from home improvements, or any other possible encroachments or what lenders call *clouds* on the title. The average cost of a title search is $154.* The cost of a title search can vary quite a bit, because some lenders merely do a quick title report that could run less than $50 whereas others may do a full title search as well as get what is called *title insurance*. Title insurance is insurance for the lender, not for you as the borrower, that there will be no challenge to the ownership rights on the real estate and that if there ever is and the challenge is successful, the loan will be paid off by the insurance policy. If title insurance is involved, the cost of that insurance varies with the loan amount, but it can range up to $300 or more. The larger the loan, the higher the title fees.

Recording Fees. Recording fees are charged by the local governmental body or recording office for the recording of the lender's lien on your property. You pay the fee to the lender who in turn records the second mortgage lien immediately following the loan closing. These fees are generally not large and range anywhere from $7 to $50.

Attorney's Fees. If the lender uses an attorney to prepare the documents and close the loan, then you will be charged for this service. Such fees average between $80 and $120.

Closing Fees. Some lenders close loans using an outside closing service or title company, and there is a fee for this service. The purpose of the closing service is to make sure that all the documents are in order and that all documents are properly signed and executed. The fee for this service is normally passed on to you and ranges between $50 and $125.

Document Preparation Fees. You may run into a document preparation fee. Usually this is part of the attorney's fee or the closing fee, but if they don't use an outside attorney nor a closing service and do the entire closing by themselves, some lenders may add on an additional cost

* op. cit.

for document preparation. In reality, however, this type of fee helps offset costs for doing the loan and may be charged in lieu of points or an application fee.

Credit Report Fee

In order for a lender to determine how strong your credit is, they will request a credit report on you. This report lists your credit history and details whether you have paid your bills, if you've ever been late with payments, and how much you've borrowed at certain lenders, department stores, or gas stations. Credit reports are described in detail in Chapter Nine on how lenders determine your credit standing. The fee can range from $5 to $50.

Lenders don't normally charge for a credit check for a home equity loan. In any case, however, the fee can be handled in one of three ways. First, as mentioned, the lender may not charge you for it at all. Or it may be included as part of the closing costs. Or it may covered by the application fee.

Usually, credit fees are non-refundable since the credit investigation has to be done and paid for whether the loan is approved or not.

Table 7-1
When Loan Fees Are Paid to the Lender

	At Application	*At Closing*	*Can Be Financed with Loan*
Application Fee	X		No
Points		X	Yes
Closing Fee		X	Yes
Check Fee		X	Yes
Credit Report Fee	X		No

When Fees Are Paid

Let's look at Table 7-1 to see the various types of one-time fees. As shown, the application fee and the credit fee are normally paid to the lender at time of application. Points, closing costs and check fees are usually paid at closing. Some lenders will, of course, deviate from this schedule, but in general this is how it will work.

Lenders will normally allow you to finance these costs because they can be quite expensive. This means these costs could become part of the loan, allowing you to pay them over time. Application fees and credit fees are usually not financed, since those fees must be paid even if the loan is not granted, and, if you don't get the loan, the lender can't very well tack these fees onto a nonexistant loan.

For example, assume that the $30,000 equity loan you're considering has an application fee of $75, points of one percent (normally called one point), which equals $300, closing costs of $144 for the appraisal plus $154 for the title, a recording fee of $10, and attorney's fees of $60 to close the loan. These costs total $743. Now that's a fair amount of money, and before you pay that you want to be pretty sure that you really want the loan. The $75 application fee is paid right up front when you apply, but that still leaves $668 that you have to pay out at time of closing. If this lender will let you finance this, you will get a check for only $29,332, which is $30,000 less the $668.

If in this example you were borrowing on a home equity line of credit, you could then draw the $668 from the equity line to pay for the closing fees. So you would start off with an initial balance of $668. In either case, the lenders like to extend you this service, because they then not only collect the fees but also interest on the fees!

Don't forget that points must be included in the APR, or Annual Percentage Rate, by regulation. If the loan rate is ten percent, the APR may well be higher due to some of these fees. Let's do an example. Assume the interest rate is ten percent on a $30,000 home equity line of credit. The APR is also ten percent as long as there are no points. Now assume that the lender charges a one-point service charge, which would be $300. The Federal government says that the lender must include the points in the calculation of the APR. If this is done, the APR now jumps to 10.18 percent.

Uncle Sam does not normally require lenders to disclose fees, such as closing costs, application fees, check fees or credit fees, as part of the APR. So it is to a lender's advantage not to charge points, which have to be disclosed. Rather, they can charge all the other fees, which don't have to be disclosed. You'll find this sort of tactic goes on in marketplaces where the competition is especially fierce. Before you sign on the dotted line, be clear what all the fees are. Specifically ask about the fees your lender mentions as well as the fees they don't mention. After all, fees can be quite high and a number of hidden fees can really raise the cost of your loan.

Ongoing Fees

Fees can also be charged periodically throughout the life of the loan. These are called ongoing fees. These fees are generally not as high as up-front fees, but they are still important because they can also be substantial. These fees include check fees, late charges, overlimit fees, returned check fees and an annual fee.

Check Fees

Check fees are found only with equity lines of credit. Since checks are not used with closed end loans, no check fees would be charged. Check fees are the cost of ordering the checks if you have check access to the equity line of credit. This fee can range anywhere from the actual cost to over $50. Be sure to find out how many checks you get. The number you receive can range up to 75. You will receive fewer than you normally would for a checking account, since you probably won't have that many transactions. This can be an ongoing cost if you use checks a lot and have to reorder at frequent intervals.

Late Fee

Late charges are fairly standard charges that are assessed to any borrower who doesn't make payments on time. These charges are covered in some detail in Chapter Twelve, and we encourage you to read about them there.

There are two basic reasons why a lender charges a late fee. One is to help cover the extra costs of collection. When a payment is late, additional costs are incurred in sending out late notices, in calls from collectors and so on. In addition, having a fee in place discourages late payments. Lenders don't want you paying late every month, because they rely on those funds coming in on time. So late fees are a combination of reimbursement for extra costs and a slap on the back of the hand to encourage you to pay on time. Individual states generally regulate late charge amounts, but they can vary from a flat amount of $5 or more each to a percentage of the payment that can result in a $30 or higher late charge.

Overlimit Fee

An overlimit fee is a fee assessed when the actual balance on an equity line of credit exceeds the line amount originally set. Not all equity lines have an overlimit fee, because it's never anticipated that the borrower will be overlimit. But let's take an example of an innocent borrower.

Assume you have a good relationship with your friendly neighborhood lender, and you've been a good customer there for a number of years. You take out a $45,000 equity line of credit, and you currently have $40,000 outstanding on your line. So you have $5,000 of credit remaining. You make a $500 payment by mail today, and then you write a check on your equity line for an emergency expense for $5,100. Before your payment is received your $5,100 check clears, and you are now $100 over your credit line.

What will your lender do? Will they go ahead and honor the check, or will they bounce the check or perhaps call you and find out what's going on? The lender may well honor your check, but because they have to do a special review and incur additional costs, the lender will probably charge an overlimit fee of perhaps $5 or $10. You can, however, call up and ask for the fee to be waived because you are a good customer. Lenders many times will waive those fees if you ask, but they will charge you if you don't mention them. Good customers are valued, but don't be a piggy about it. If you have more than one late payment per year, you deserve the charge.

Returned Check Fee

If you make a payment and your check is returned for Not Sufficient Funds (NSF), then many lenders will charge you a return payment fee. This could result in a double charge for you if the institution where you keep the checking account also charges you a fee. Together, these fees could add up to quite a bit, perhaps as high as $50. So know if there is a returned-check fee and how much it is.

Annual Fee

Those of you who have credit cards are probably familiar with annual fees. Many credit cards have annual fees which you must pay to the lender once a year for the privilege of having the credit card. Many equity lines of credit also have annual fees. The fee amount ranges from $15 to more than $100. Before you take out an equity line of credit, know if the lender has an annual fee and how much it is. If the lender charges an annual fee but waives application fees and points, that may be an acceptable trade-off. However, if the lender charges an application fee plus points plus an annual fee, then start walking. In today's competitive marketplace, lenders often can be found that charge only one or two of the fees but not all three.

Trade-off between Fees and Rate

The critical aspect of fees is their effect on your wallet. How do they affect price? How do they relate to the most familiar part of price, the interest rate? Are you better off having higher fees and a lower rate or a higher rate and lower fees? The answers to these questions are "a lot," "a lot" and "it depends." This is a very important consideration, so let's take a closer look at these questions.

The trade-off between fees and rate depends to a large extent upon your use. If you're taking out an equity line of credit that you don't intend to use for some time or for only a short period of time, you would be better off with no fees up front and a higher rate. The same is true if you're taking out any equity loan that you plan to pay off before the full term. For example, if you're doing some repairs in anticipation of selling

Table 7-2
Tradeoff between Rate and Fees
$30,000 Equity Line, 10 Years

	Loan A *9.5% Rate—High Fees*	Loan B *10.0% Rate—No Fees*
Application Fee	$75.00	$0.00
Points (1%)	$300.00	$0.00
Disclosed APR	9.68%	10.00%
Closing Costs	$300.00	$0.00
Annual Fee	$20.00	$0.00
Effective Rate with All Fees	10.00%	10.00%
Prepay Loan in Two Years	10.86%	10.00%

your property within a year or two, you're better off paying a higher rate and lower fees. Fees are calculated to give the lender a certain yield for the full term of the loan, which may be five, ten, or even 15 years. But if you shorten that term by prepaying, then the fees become a greater percentage of the total finance charge, and the yield rises for the lender.

An example can clarify the trade-off between fees and interest rate. Two loans are shown in Table 7-2. Loan A has a 9.5 percent interest rate with high fees. Loan B has a higher rate, ten percent, but there are no fees because of a special sale. Now, how do the two loans really compare?

Let's look at Loan A first. The fees include an application fee of $75, one point which on a $30,000 line would be $300, closing costs which include costs for the title, the appraisal, the recording, and any closing fees for a total of $300 and an annual fee of $20. Now which would you rather have, the 9.5 percent loan with the fees or the ten percent loan with no fees? Surprisingly, both loans provide the same yield, or effective rate, to the lender. This may not be a great surprise, because you probably had a feeling we were setting you up. In other words, the lender's yield is ten percent on the ten percent loan with no fees, because that is what the interest rate is. But on the 9.5 percent loan, while the interest rate is 9.5 percent, the fees yield an extra one-half of one percent, so this lender will also make ten percent on the loan.

So are there any differences in price between the two loans? Yes, there are. First, if you don't draw the entire line of $30,000, Loan B with no fees but a higher rate is more economical for you. The reason for this is that Loan B at ten percent generates only interest for the lender, and if the full balance is not outstanding then there is less interest income.

Second, if you prepay, Loan B is again more economical. If you draw the full $30,000 line but only keep it out for two years, Loan B with the ten percent rate earns ten percent for two years on the money that is out there and that is all. But Loan A has already earned all those high fees up front. That loan's profitability depends much more heavily on the fees, and those fees were calculated on a ten-year term. If you prepay in two years, the yield to the lender jumps to 10.86 percent. And as the yield to the lender increases, that means you pay more.

Ultimately the trade-off between the loan rate and the fees depends on how you're going to use the loan and how long you're going to keep it. On an equity line that you plan to use little or on a closed end loan that you plan to pay off early, stick with the higher rate and lower fees. Of course, the best of both worlds is a lower rate and lower fees. Does that ever happen? Sure it does. Just watch your local papers. Like the gas wars of 20 years ago, price wars also happen in financial products. If you're a smart shopper, you can come out ahead on this type of deal.

Variable Rate Considerations

Whether your loan is closed end or open end, there are some important things to consider if you accept a variable rate. Among the most important considerations are the index and the spread over the index. You need to know the spread over the index because that tells you what is really going to happen to your monthly payment amount. Let's look at those considerations now.

Indexing

An *index* is a base rate upon which changes in your loan rate are determined. Some common examples of an index are the prime lending rate of banks, the Treasury bill rate, the Federal Home Loan Bank cost of funds rate and internal indexes. A lender uses one of these rates as a base index and then attaches a spread over that rate to determine your loan rate. These indexes are explained in detail below.

Prime Rate Index. Prime rate is a fairly common index for open end loans. It is the loan rate at which the big banks are willing to lend to their big corporate borrowers.

Your loan would not be at prime (unless you were a big corporate borrower!) but at a spread over prime, such as two percent to four percent over prime. Therefore, if the prime rate is eight percent and the spread is four percent, then your loan rate would be 12 percent.

Prime can be a good index to use from your perspective. First, it's well known and very easy to find. Most metropolitan newspapers as well as the *Wall Street Journal* publish the prime rate daily. And since prime is a major money index, any time the prime changes there are usually announcements on television and radio. Secondly, prime doesn't change as often as other rates do. Therefore, it can be a stable index which is not as susceptible to minor ups and downs as are other indexes.

However, it is a somewhat arbitrary figure, set internally by the big banks. Thus, it is to some degree an administered rate rather than a market rate, although it is based on the general cost of money in the marketplace.

Treasury Bill Rate Index. A good index using the actual market cost of money is the Treasury bill rate. Treasury bills are issued by the United States Treasury Department to help fund the spending of the country. Treasury bills are sold at an auction held by the Treasury Department every Tuesday, so these rates change on Tuesday. Treasury bills, or T-bills as they are commonly called, come in different maturities, and the rate is based on the maturity. So there is a 1-month T-bill rate, a 3-month T-bill rate and so on. The longer the maturity, generally the higher the rate. So if your lender uses a T-bill rate, you need to know which T-bill. The 3-month T-bill, or 13-week T-bill, is most commonly used.

Your spread over the 3-month T-bill rate will be at least 3.5 percent. The T-bill rate is lower than prime, so the spread or what you pay over

Chart 7-3
Ten-Year Annual Average History of Two Common Lending Indexes

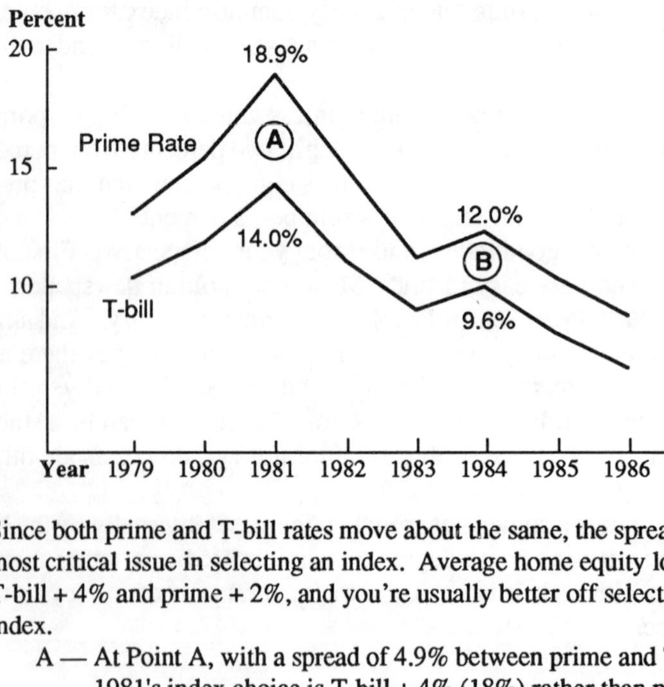

Since both prime and T-bill rates move about the same, the spread is the most critical issue in selecting an index. Average home equity loan rates are T-bill + 4% and prime + 2%, and you're usually better off selecting a T-bill index.

A — At Point A, with a spread of 4.9% between prime and T-bill, 1981's index choice is T-bill + 4% (18%) rather than prime + 2% (20.9%).

B — At Point B, although the spread is only 2.4%, prime + 2% (14%) is still more expensive than T-bill + 4% (13.6%), and you would still choose the T-bill index.

the T-bill rate will usually be greater than the spread used with the prime rate.

The T-bill rate is a good index because it is also very easy to find in metropolitan newspapers as well as the *Wall Street Journal*. However, since it reflects more closely the actual cost of money in the marketplace, this rate will change weekly at the time of the Treasury Department auction. If your loan rate is subject to change quarterly, which is the most common, you can expect it to actually change whereas a rate based on prime may not change from quarter to quarter.

We said that prime is an administered rate based on the lending institution's cost of money while the T-bill rate is a money market rate. Do they therefore differ significantly? No, they actually follow each other quite closely on an annual basis. Chart 7-3 shows a ten-year history of the prime rate as compared to the 3-month T-bill rate. The rate shown for each year is an average for that year. Note it is possible that the prime rate had only a few changes within that year whereas the T-bill rate could have changed up to 52 times. Look at how the two rates move in relation to each other. Prime rate will always be higher than the 3- month T-bill rate, but notice that the spread between prime and the T-bill rate stays fairly constant. Lenders will charge an average of two percent over prime, meaning that if prime is nine percent your loan rate is 11 percent. And they charge an average of four percent over the T-bill rate, meaning that if the T-bill rate is seven percent your rate is still 11 percent. However, if you look closely at the table, you see there have been times when the T-bill rate approached prime, meaning that if your index were the T-bill rate, you may be paying more than someone with the prime rate as an index. Overall, the T-bill rate may change more often but is less volatile than prime, and therefore this rate would be preferred as an index.

FHLBB Cost of Funds Rate Index. The Federal Home Loan Bank Board Cost of Funds rate, or what is commonly called the FHLBB cost of funds rate, is a rate set by each of the 12 FHLBB districts and reflects the average cost of funds for savings and loans within that district. There is also a national average rate, but the district rate is commonly used. This rate is primarily used for adjustable rate first mortgages, but it is also used for second mortgages, especially by savings and loans.

The FHLBB cost of funds rate changes monthly and so can be the least volatile of the three rates discussed here, since the T-bill rate is subject to change weekly and prime is subject to change at any time. However, the FHLBB cost of funds is an average rate of all the deposits at a savings and loan which includes high-cost long-term funds, and therefore can be a higher cost to you.

Internal Rate Index. This is a rate that lenders set and change internally based on their own formulas or discretion. While this index may be very workable for lenders and reflect their true cost of funds, an internal rate index can be very uncomfortable for consumers. This is especially true if the rate is changed arbitrarily. And most financial institutions that use internal rate indexes do indeed change the rate "whenever the Chairman decides." And remember, most Chairmen drive Cadillacs for which someone has paid.

If your variable rate loan is tied to an internal index, be very careful to find out what the formula is that is used by the institution. If they can't explain it, you may want to reconsider whether their low rate is worth it. You may decide you prefer a rate that is somewhat higher initially but that is tied to an unbiased third party rate, such as prime or T-bills.

Negative Amortization

Danger number two is negative amortization. Negative amortization means that, instead of your principal decreasing with each payment, your principal will increase. How can this happen?

This situation is unusual with a line of credit home equity loan, but it can happen in the following way. Let's say your minimum payment is one percent per month. That equates to 12 percent per year. If your interest rate rises above 12 percent per year and you keep paying one percent per month, you aren't paying enough to cover interest, and your principal won't reduce.

Negative amortization is much more likely to be encountered with a variable rate fixed term loan. To illustrate, assume you've borrowed $15,000 at 12 percent for ten years or 120 months. When you first start paying back the loan, only a small portion of your payment will go toward the principal. In this example, your payment is $215.21. The first month, $65.21 or 30 percent goes toward reducing the principal while

$150 or 70 percent pays the accumulated interest. And the last month, $213.08 goes toward reducing the principal while $2.13 pays the interest due.

Now, assume your interest rate climbs six percent to 18 percent, a not unreasonable possibility. The interest due for the first payment is now $225, so your payment of $215.21 is $9.79 short. Lenders that allow negative amortization take the extra $9.79 and add it to your principal. This is called *capitalization.* Your interest will then be considered to be paid for that month, but your principal, instead of decreasing to $14,934.79, has now risen to $15,009.79. If interest rates stay at 18 percent and you keep paying $215.21, by the end of the term, instead of your principal being paid off, you will now owe $18,185.73! And that isn't all the bad news. Since the extra $9.79 is now part of your principal, you will have to pay interest on it for the next month. So you are in effect paying interest on interest. This is a very high price to pay for the comfort of a fixed payment amount.

Caps and Floors

One way to protect yourself against unmanageable rate increases when you consider a variable rate loan is to get one that offers a good rate and has a cap. A *cap* is the maximum by which an interest rate can increase over a certain length of time. In the past, many home equity (or second mortgage) loans didn't have caps, or the caps were not revealed because it wasn't required. However, new legislation in 1987 stated that all lenders must disclose caps. This law does not set any specific limits on caps but does stipulate that the lender must disclose what the cap is.

In a sense, this has a self-regulating effect. It would not be wise for a lender to disclose a cap of 20 percent, which would allow a loan rate to rise from nine percent to 29 percent. While technically that could have happened in the days when there were no caps or they did not have to be disclosed, most people applying for variable rate loans did not consider how high their interest rate could go. Now when the cap is disclosed, lenders are alerting potential borrowers to the fact that their loan rates can go up and by how much they could go up. So the legislation does put pressure on lenders to set reasonable caps on home equity loans.

Let's look at an example using caps. In mortgage loans, and in home equity loans, it is very common to have a cap of two percent per year and a lifetime cap of six percent, meaning that whatever the base rate is, it can never increase more than two percent per year and six percent total over the original rate. Using the example of 9.5 percent for an equity loan, if you had a six percent cap, then that 9.5 percent could increase by two percent per year but never to more than 15.5 percent. Once the rate reached 15.5 percent, the rate would never go higher even if the lender's index were higher. You see that you have some interest rate risk, but it is limited to a maximum level, so you would always know what the worst-case scenario could be. If you can't afford the monthly payments at the maximum interest rate that your lender can charge you, then you should either borrow a smaller amount or shop for a fixed rate loan you can afford.

How do you know what that maximum payment could be? One way, of course, is to ask your lender. This must be disclosed to you with some loan types but not all. But even if your lender lets you down and won't tell you, we will. Because the other way is to look in the back of this book where the appendix presents a Monthly Payment Calculator showing what the monthly payments are at various interest rates. This Payment Calculator shows rates from seven percent to 16 percent and covers terms of five years, ten years, 15 years and 20 years for every $1,000 of a loan. To calculate what your monthly payment is, find the rate at the side of the chart and the term at the top of the chart. Where the two intersect in the body of the table is the factor you need. Multiply that factor by the number of thousands of dollars you are borrowing.

For example, at a nine percent rate for ten years, the payment is $12.67 per $1,000. If you borrowed $10,000, your payment would be $12.67 times ten, or $126.70 per month. Although the Monthly Payment Calculator is accurate within a few cents, rounding errors will appear in your payment calculation at higher loan amounts such as $75,000. But in general this Payment Calculator will allow you to figure what the payment range will be.

Caps are often accompanied by *floors*. Floors are set limits restricting how low the rate can go. Unlike caps, floors are not regulated. Just as caps protect the consumer, floors protect the lender. If particular lenders don't have floors and rates drop lower than what they are comfortable with, they cannot change their minds and impose a floor at a later date. But they can change terms and conditions on amounts yet to be borrowed from credit lines. Then, as a borrower, it is your choice to decide whether you want to borrow more money under the new conditions.

Like a cap, a floor can be expressed as a percent, such as two percent per year and six percent lifetime. To be most equitable to the consumer, a floor should approximate the cap. So if a lender has a lifetime cap of six percent, then the floor should be about the same. For example, a cap of eight percent and a floor of two percent is unfair to the consumer. Here, lenders want to protect themselves to allow rates to go up eight percent but will only give you the benefit of rates going down two percent. A floor can also be expressed as a flat interest rate, such as "no lower than 5.5 percent." Again using the example above, the cap may be six percent and the floor may be stated to be five percent. So starting from your initial borrowing rate of 9.5 percent, the interest rate could never go higher than 15.5 percent nor lower than 4.5 percent.

Not all lenders have a floor. Some lenders set no limit on the extent by which rates can go down. Pratically speaking, however, don't ever count on your rate decreasing to three percent or two percent. Five percent is a realistic floor and most homeowners would be more than happy to have a loan rate of 4.5 percent or 5.5 percent. Floors are certainly logical. Therefore, you want to look for a lender that will allow the rate to be reduced by at least four percent.

When comparing floors of one lender with another, keep the relative level in mind. In other words, if your rate would be 11.5 percent and the floor is four percent, your rate could only go down to 7.5 percent. And that's not good enough. For a rate of 11.5 percent, you want a floor of six percent, allowing your interest rate to go down to 5.5 percent.

Strategies

By understanding the pricing of a home equity loan, you will be able to make the best deal for yourself. Taking a second mortgage on your home that will probably last anywhere from five to fifteen years is no trivial step and is worthy of some of your time and effort to make sure it's done right. By understanding the pricing, you will save yourself a lot of money. Here are some of our thoughts on appropriate pricing.

Since a variable rate tied to an internal index can change up or down "whenever the Chairman decides," stay away from it unless you are the Chairman!

We also feel negative amortization can be a real trap, especially if interest rates rise as high as they did in the early 1980s. Negative amortization is usually a trade-off for more stable monthly payments. But think about it; do you really achieve stability if the payment remains the same but the balance increases? We think you don't and recommend that you avoid any programs that include negative amortization.

Some fees and costs are variable and will cost more the higher you go on the loan amount. Points and title charges are examples of these. And remember, you pay these charges based on the line amount, not the amount you may need. So if you take out a line for $60,000 when you only need $30,000, you are paying fees on that additional $30,000, even though you may never use it. This is a good argument for taking a line amount only for what you feel you really need.

When comparing fees versus APR, keep in mind that if you plan to prepay a loan before its full term is up, then you are better off taking a slightly higher rate with lower fees.

Don't let fees be a surprise at closing. Watch out for "hidden fees." These are fees not disclosed up front or not included in the advertising. More about this in Chapter Ten on shopping for a home equity loan.

If you choose a variable rate loan, know the caps and floors involved. Caps protect you and floors protect the lender. Watch out for unreasonable caps. Rates can change quickly, and you will have to live with that cap for a long time.

Chapter Eight

Other Considerations:
Payment Methods, Insurance, Payoff

While the cost of your loan is certainly important, there are other features you need to know about to be fully informed and avoid as many mistakes as possible. For example, how can you repay your loan? And what about that insurance the lenders keep trying to sell you? What happens if you want to refinance? What if, at the end of the term of a home equity line of credit, you still have a substantial balance outstanding? You need to know what your options are in all of these cases.

Payment Methods

Home equity loans can be repaid in a variety of different ways. Repayment methods tend to fall into two categories: those used for open end lines of credit (similar to a credit card) and those used for closed end loans (similar to an auto loan).

Closed End Loans

Closed end loans tend to have simple payment techniques. The fixed rate closed end loan is the simplest of all. Consumers make a payment of a fixed amount every month throughout the life of the loan. But payments on a variable rate closed end loan normally will vary. How often a payment may change is a function of how often the rate changes. And this rate change can be reflected in two ways.

The most common method to reflect a rate change is to vary the payment. So if your rate goes up two percent, your payment may go from \$238 a month to \$267 per month. However, many consumers fear that their payments may go higher than they can afford. To alleviate this fear, another method of reflecting rate change has appeared. This method keeps the amount of the payment the same but lengthens or shortens the term. So if rates go up, instead of the payment increasing, the loan term may be extended from 60 months to 63 months. The borrower would have three additional payments to make up for the rise in interest rate. On the other hand, if the interest rates were to drop, the borrower would have fewer payments. While we have seen some of these loans, they haven't really caught on, primarily due to the supply side of the market, the lenders. Fixed term adjustable payment is the common approach, and it is readily acceptable in the secondary market. Lenders who make loans with the idea of selling them at some point in time try to structure them to make them attractive, or at least acceptable, to the secondary market. And the secondary market doesn't like variable terms. Also, another consideration is that it can be difficult to find a computer system that can handle the variable term loan.

Open End Loans

Open end home equity lines of credit offer various types of repayment options. Consumers can repay interest only, a percentage of principal plus interest, or a fixed amount.

Interest only is used by about ten percent of lenders in the market today. Under this method, borrowers can pay only the interest while principal reduction is not required as part of the minimum monthly payment. Borrowers can, of course, pay as much principal as they want, but they don't have to. Under the interest-only plan, monthly payments tend to be quite low. The danger with this option is that consumers may be tempted to borrow more than they can really afford to repay. At some point in time the principal must be paid, and with an interest-only loan you may be stuck with paying the full principal in one lump sum at the end of the term.

A more common method is to pay a percentage of principal and interest. This is similar to a credit card where you repay a certain percentage of your principal and the interest outstanding. For example, if you had a $30,000 credit line that was fully drawn down and which therefore had a $30,000 outstanding balance, you may have a principal and interest payment of one-and-one-half percent per month. One-and-one-half percent of $30,000 would be $450 per month. All of the interest outstanding would be paid from this $450, and whatever is remaining would then go toward reducing the principal. This is a very common repayment scheme, and is probably familiar to you.

The danger with this repayment option is that if you pay only the minimum due and your line is fully drawn, you may never pay off the principal and may again be stuck with a balloon payment at the end of the term. So look closely at what the minimum percentage is. Anything less than about 4.5 percent may not fully amortize a loan in 120 months. Also, even if you pay an adequate amount to fully amortize the loan or to fully pay it off by the end of the term, you could still redraw the money toward the end of the term. And then you would still have a large balance to pay off in a short period of time. So be very careful of a plan that requires you to pay only a small minimum; there may be a hidden, and very serious, danger.

There is a variation to this repayment scheme. The loan may stipulate that you pay one-and-one-half percent of the principal plus the interest. Using the example above, the difference here is that the $450 payment would go toward only the principal. You would then have to pay the interest in addition. So your total payment would be higher but is more likely to amortize the loan. When you're exploring payment options, be sure to ask whether the minimum percentage payment is a percentage of principal and interest or just a percentage of principal with the interest added to the payment. A payment that is structured as a percentage of principal plus the interest increases your payment amount by about 50 percent.

The third payment method is a fixed payment. Here, the lender specifies a fixed payment amount regardless of the amount of the balance. So the payment amount would be constant throughout the life of the loan. Whether your balance is $10,000 or $700, your monthly payment would still be, say, $300 per month. This payment option holds some comfort for consumers concerned about a payment that changes and therefore affects budgeting. However, the one concern with a fixed payment is that if interest rates get very high on a variable rate loan, your payment could be insufficient to cover even the interest expense and would certainly not cover the principal. Therefore, your loan would be subject to negative amortization where your principal balance would increase rather than decrease, because your payment is not even sufficient to cover interest.

Automatic Debit

Whichever payment method you choose, some lenders allow you to (or you may be forced to accept!) an automatic debit. This is an automatic deduction of your payment, for whatever amount that is, from a savings or checking account. The automatic debit requires that you have a transaction account at your lender's institution, or possibly a payroll deduction account which is popular at credit unions. This is usually a checking account, but it could be a savings or a money market type of account. On the payment due date, the lender's computer automatically deducts the money from your transaction account or debits your account and deposits that amount as a payment to your equity loan.

The advantage of an automatic debit is convenience. The borrower doesn't have to worry about making out a check, putting a stamp on the letter, putting it in the mail and getting it there on time. You save the time, effort and postage of having to make the payment every month, because you know it is automatically deducted from your account. An additional plus is the fact that it may cost less. When a lender must collect the payment in the normal way, it can cost up to $8 or more per month to cover the processing of a mail payment. The mailroom must be staffed with people to open the payments, sort them, process the checks, and apply them to the account, and the checks must be cleared through the clearing house. So a mail payment goes through many hands, is time consuming and is expensive. The cost saving of an automatic debit over manual handling of a mail payment can be as high as $5 per payment. For a 120-month loan, this saves the lender $600. Because of this savings, some lenders offer a discount if the borrower accepts an automatic debit program. This savings can take the form of free checking or a reduced interest rate, which is normally between one-eight to one-fourth of a percentage point.

However, this feature also has disadvantages. Most important, borrowers aren't able to take advantage of the float. If your payment is due on the first of the month, you may write the check on the tenth knowing that the late charge is not assessed until the fifteenth of the month. This is playing the float. If you have an automatic debit, your account would be debited on the due date and you would lose the ten-day float that you otherwise would have. Automatic debits also have a disadvantage if the loan has a variable rate or if it is an equity line. In this case, the borrower may not have a set monthly payment and so would not know, until the statement is received, exactly the amount that was debited. A way around this is to use a lender that sets a fixed monthly payment even on variable rate loans or lines of credit.

In general, we believe that an automatic debit is a good idea. We all get a little grumpy when we have to pay bills each month. We would much rather have payments automatically taken out of our accounts than to have to take the time to write out all the checks, sort them, put them in envelopes, put postage on the envelopes, try to get to the post office before noon on Saturday and then be grumpy for the rest of the day.

Credit Insurance

One of the choices you are certain to be faced with as a potential user of an equity line of credit or a home equity loan is whether or not you want to include credit insurance as part of your financial package. This feature is becoming increasingly common, and just about any type of loan you take out will come with credit insurance. But just how useful is credit insurance? What does it really cost? And do the costs justify the benefits?

There are three basic types of credit insurance—single credit life insurance, joint credit life insurance and disability insurance.

Credit Life Insurance

Life insurance is exactly that—insurance on your life. Credit life insures that in case you die, your loan will be paid off by the insurance. This provides protection to the lender that they will get their money back, and it provides protection to your spouse or other dependents that they will not be burdened with paying your loan back.

The basic choice for credit life is between single life and joint life. Single credit life insurance covers one person on the loan, who may be the principal borrower or the principal wage earner. Joint credit life, however, covers co-borrowers on the loan, such as a husband and wife.

Credit life insures closed end loans and open end loans in slightly different ways. Let's examine both ways. Principal on a closed end home equity loan is repaid in a fixed amount per month for the term of the loan. This loan would then have a declining principal balance. For this loan, a declining balance insurance is used to match the liability. Each month, as you make your payment, your outstanding balance is reduced, and your insurance is reduced as well. So if you borrowed $20,000, at the beginning of the first month you would be insured for $20,000. But by the seventh year of the loan when the balance is only $3,000, the insurance would only cover $3,000.

An equity line of credit, on the other hand, has payments that can vary from month to month, and your balance may also have wide swings from month to month. In this case, the insurance is more complicated. You have two choices. The first type of coverage covers the exact amount you owe. If your equity line of credit balance were $17,320 and you died, then the insurance would pay off $17,320. The second type of coverage is actually a term-life policy where you arc insured for the term of the loan for the full amount of the line whether you take it all out or not. If you had a $20,000 equity line of credit and the term was ten years, you would receive a term insurance policy of $20,000 for ten years. If you were to die at any time during that ten years, your beneficiaries would receive $20,000, regardless of the outstanding balance on the equity line of credit.

This second type of insurance for equity lines is fairly new. Although it is just starting to come on the market in conjunction with a loan, it has been around for a long time as a product. The insurance previously found with loans was always declining balance; now the market is starting to offer term life.

Disability Insurance

Disability insurance covers the primary insured for any disability that keeps him or her from being gainfully employed and therefore earning an income to make the loan payments. Normally, disability insurance covers only one person even if you have joint life insurance. And the person covered is automatically the primary insured. This means the principal wage earner; however, in two-income families this should be specified at loan closing. Disability insurance covers all the payments while the primary insured is disabled. So if your payments are $264 a month, then the disability insurance will make those payments of $264 a month for you during the time when you cannot. Once you return to work and are no longer disabled, then the payments must again be made by you.

Disability insurance can work in a variety of different ways. The two main types are retroactive insurance and elimination insurance. As an example for retroactive insurance, assume a 14-day retroactive disability insurance. This means that you must be out of work for at least 14 continuous days before you can file a claim. On the 15th day of continuous disability you may file a claim, but because this is retroactive insurance the claim amount paid will be retroactive to your first day of disability. This type of insurance protects the insurance carrier from minor illnesses, such as colds or flu, which require absences of three days or so but protects borrowers from having to bear any cost if they are truly disabled or out of work for any extended time.

Elimination insurance also has a waiting period. So, for example, you may again file a claim for insurance on the 15th day of your disability. But elimination insurance will only cover you from the 15th day on; there is no retroactive feature. So you lose the first two weeks. While elimination insurance may not seem as good a bargain as retroactive insurance, elimination insurance is usually cheaper.

The most common insurance types for accident or disability insurance are seven-day retroactive, 14-day retroactive, and 30-day retroactive, and 14-day elimination, and 30-day elimination. The most expensive insurance, as you may guess, is the seven-day retroactive, because you have to be disabled the least number of days and it pays all the way back to day one. The least expensive insurance is 30-day elimination, because you must be out of work for the longest number of days and you must pay the first 30 days by yourself.

Insurance Premiums and Costs

How do you pay for insurance and what does it cost? Answering the last question first, credit insurance costs vary from state to state, so an exact amount cannot be provided. Each state regulates its own schedule of charges, so no matter what figure we gave you, we would only be right one out of 50 times.

Paying for insurance on a home equity loan follows two basic methods. The first method is single payment insurance. This is most commonly found with closed end fixed rate loans. The premium for the full term of the loan is calculated and paid up front as a single lump sum. Usually this amount is financed, and you don't have to come up with the cash.

The second method is more common for variable rate loans and equity lines of credit. This is where the premium is paid basically on a month-to-month basis. Each month, when you get your statement, the insurance is added to the payment.

The final decision on whether to take credit life or disability insurance is up to you. It is often said that it's cheaper to get credit insurance from your own insurance agent. Getting this type of insurance on your own could take more time and effort than it's worth. Simply getting a quote from your own insurance agent might be worth it, however. You should ask for something quite inexpensive, and you could even include the cost of the premiums in your loan request.

What Happens at the End of the Loan?

When you approach the end of the term of your loan, there are various things that can happen. For closed end loans, the options are quite simple: you let the loan go to maturity, or you refinance before the end of the term. Open end loans have more options. All of these are discussed below.

Closed End Loans That Go to Term

Closed end loans are paid off by the end of the loan term, so if you let your loan go to term, at the end of the term your loan balance should be zero. The only thing that happens at the end of the term of a closed end home equity loan is that your lender should provide you with a release deed releasing their security interest in your property as well as the original note you signed and the mortgage showing that it's cancelled or has been paid off. Once you receive this release document, you should check to make sure it has been filed with the local filing office, because the release must be recorded. Many lenders will do this for you for a fee. Others will send you the release and let you know that you must do that yourself. Either way, it is a mistake to simply file the release in a drawer to look at in the future. We would bet high stakes that what will happen is that it won't be done, and then ten years later, if you try to sell your house, this old security interest will show up as an open lien. The chances of you going back into that same drawer and finding that release deed from the lender are quite remote. And the chances of the institution still having a copy of the release deed in their own files are even more remote, because they destroy those files after a reasonable time. So be sure your release deed is recorded.

Refinancing a Closed End Loan

You do have another option. What if you decide you want to refinance before the end of the term? For example, assume that you borrowed $15,000 four years ago for some major remodeling on your house. Your loan rate was 12 percent, but the total fees you paid including title and appraisal effectively increased the loan rate to 12.50 percent. The original term was ten years resulting in a monthly payment of $215.21.

Now you decide that you want to do some more work for an additional $8,000. The first choice is to refinance your existing loan by borrowing the $8,000 plus enough to pay off your current second mortgage of $11,111.98. The total loan would now be $19,111.98. But this is not a wise move. Here's why:

1. Your principal balance outstanding is $11,111.98, so, while 40 percent of the loan period is over, you have not paid off 40 percent of the balance. As you should know by now, more interest is paid at the beginning of the loan. In this case, your payments are just about at the point where you begin to pay more toward the principal than the interest. And now you want to start over?
2. Your original loan had a rate of 12 percent that was effectively increased to 12.50 percent due to the fees you had to pay. The

extra .5 percent was based on a ten-year term, but when you shorten it to a four-year term, the cost to you goes up to 12.72 percent.

3. When you refinance you will probably be required to pay fees again based on the full amount of the refinanced loan—the $8,000 new amount and the $11,111 to pay off the old loan. Since you already paid fees on the old amount of $11,111 once four years ago, you are in effect having to pay double fees on more than half of what you are borrowing.

What are your options in such a case? There are four that you can consider:

1. Keep the loan and do not borrow anything more until it is paid off.
2. Find a lender who will make a third mortgage loan and not require the second to be paid off. Be cautious of the rate, however, as some lenders dealing in third mortgages can have very high rates.
3. You could have taken out an equity line of credit in the first place and then have drawn more funds as needed.
4. Negotiate with the lender who has your existing second mortgage loan for a lower rate and a waiver of fees on the "old money" or, in this case, the $11,111. After all, they aren't really giving you the $11,111. They already gave that to you four years ago. Now they're only moving numbers from one account to another. Your lender really only has to come up with $8,000 in new cash. So you should only have to pay fees on $8,000.

In summary, then, before you decide to refinance an existing closed end home equity loan, be careful how much it might cost you.

Open End Loans

Open end loans are more complicated. First, these borrowers should also receive a release of security at the end of the term, and they need to make sure it's recorded. But the primary thing that happens at the end of the term of an open end loan is the disposition of any outstanding balances. By its very nature, an open end line of credit allows you to make draws at any point in time, and, if you had a ten-year line of credit, you could draw out the full amount on the ninth year and 11th month. There is, of course, no way to amortize that within one month, so when the loan matures you would have the full principal to pay off. So now what do you do? It's up to you and the lender and the original agreement you signed as to what you're allowed to do. You really have three alternatives, which are discussed below.

Pay It Off in Full. The lender may require you to make full payment of any outstanding balance. In this case, you could go to another lender and get another equity line or perhaps a closed end loan with which to pay off the balance. If this is going to be your option, you need to decide before the term is expired. You can't wait until the day that the loan matures to decide to go somewhere else to borrow the money to pay it off; you can't get an equity loan approved in one day. Contact your lender about 60 days before the loan expires and find out what they are going to do. If the lender requires the loan to be paid off, you can then inquire whether they wish to be the one to refinance the existing balance if you don't pay it off. This needs to be negotiated between you and your lender at least two months before the expiration date of your line of credit.

Refinance through the Existing Lender. Many lenders will offer a refinance in the form of a term loan at time of expiration. About one or two months prior to expiration they will send you a letter stating that your full balance will be due and payable soon, but, if you don't wish to pay it all off, they will be happy to refinance it for you using a standard closed end second mortgage. Be forewarned that you will have to pay fees for the refinancing. And a new loan rate will apply.

You don't have to wait until the maturity date to roll over your loan. If you are in the eighth or ninth year of a ten-year equity line of credit and you have the full balance outstanding, you probably already know that you are going to have to refinance it through a closed end loan that amortizes. In this case, you may want to take advantage of a period of low interest rates and refinance it early. If rates come down to eight percent or nine percent and you feel that they may go up next year, then it may be to your advantage to refinance the line even before it expires.

Roll Over the Existing Account. Some lenders will offer the option of rolling over your credit line for an additional term such as three, five, or even ten more years. There are fees involved in doing this because they will probably do another cursory credit check to see if your credit standing has changed. They will also need to record the mortgage again since the first security lien has expired, which involves an appraisal to see if the market value of your home has changed, a title search to see if any liens have been attached in the meantime, and all the rest. The fees will approximate the fees you paid for the first loan.

Refinancing your line of credit into a term loan or rolling over the remaining balance into a new equity line is very much to your current lender's advantage. First, your current lender may be able and willing to refinance for less than a new institution since they know you and they already have some documentation on your property. Also, if you have been a good borrower, meaning that you've made your payments on time with no problems, they already know they would be lending the money to a good credit risk. Also, it costs a lot of money to get new accounts to sign up for equity lines of credit whereas you have already proved to be a good paying customer.

Strategies

We have some definite ideas on the care and feeding of your home equity loan. First, we recommend using a checkbook to access your equity line of credit. This provides sufficient control but also allows a degree of both flexibility and convenience.

For payments, we like the automatic debit, because its convenience offsets any float loss. But you should also try to get a price discount from your lender for using this method.

Credit insurance can offer some peace of mind, but you will need to determine yourself what that is worth. Also, the structures you will encounter may be unfamiliar to you, and the pricing may appear strange, so shop carefully.

Knowing what will happen at the end of your loan term on an equity line of credit is a biggie. Waiting until one month before the loan expires is too late. Find out now while shopping for a suitable lender.

Be careful of refinances on a closed end equity loan. That is how lenders can get rich. Use our suggestions to save yourself money if you are considering a refinance.

Chapter Nine

Your House and Your Credit: *How Do They Stack Up?*

Welcome to the chapter on credit analysis. We're going to take you behind the scenes, to the other side of that door where few consumers are allowed. You'll have the opportunity to peek into the inner sanctum of a lender's underwriting department and see what kind of magic is used to decide whether or not you get the loan and how much you get.

You may be disappointed to find that there's really not that much magic to it. Although your lender may not be willing to admit it, lending decisions are basically common sense with a few empirically derived formulas and ratios. Remember what we said at the beginning of the book? The authors have a wealth of experience in not only making these loans themselves but also in training lenders just how to do this, the underwriting of your loan. So get ready to proceed into the loan underwriting department to see exactly what goes on.

The Appraisal

In order to qualify for a home equity loan, you must of course own a home and then have some equity in it. Without both of these requirements you'll surely fail to get that home equity loan. Don't laugh. We've heard of apartment dwellers applying for this loan.

Let's assume that you do own your home. You have a title and a deed to the home and not just a contract to buy. So how much is your home worth? We all have a feeling about how much our home is worth, but that's not necessarily supported by the real marketplace. So lenders must make an appraisal, an estimate of what your home would be worth on the open market. This allows them to calculate how much they can lend you. And since an appraisal is usually a requirement for a home equity loan, the lender will arrange to have an appraiser come by to appraise your home.

There are several different types of appraisals that can be done. Some are brief where the appraiser may not even walk into your home. Others are extremely detailed, and, after the appraiser has visited your house, he or she may take a long time to write up the appraisal. If your lender has any intention of selling your loan to the secondary market (which is likely if it's a closed end loan), the long form of appraisal is required. And this means more expense for you, since you're most likely paying for the appraisal, and a longer time to wait for the completed appraisal.

The three basic approaches to valuing a residence are replacement cost, market analysis and income approach.

When using the replacement-cost method, the appraiser calculates the square footage of your dwelling, taking into consideration the number of bedrooms, the number of baths, etc., and, based on its location, estimates what it would cost on a dollar-per-square-foot basis to replace your property. Once this dollar amount is calculated, then a deduction is made for wear and tear if your home is not brand new.

In the second approach, the market analysis, the appraiser compares your home to others that have recently been sold. For example, if you have a two-story, three-bedroom, two-bath home, appraisers would look for sales of comparable houses in the same neighborhood or houses within as close a distance to your home as possible. They then adjust the prices at which those other homes were sold for the features that are different. For example, if the comparable home had five bedrooms instead of three, appraisers would deduct some amount for the lesser number of bedrooms in order to make the two homes comparable. This adjustment allows the appraiser to estimate the market value of your home if it were to be sold on the open market. The average sales price of three properties is generally used to compare to your home.

The third type of appraisal is the income approach, used primarily for multi-family, income-producing dwellings rather than single-family homes. In this approach, the income from the building is used to derive an economic value for the building based on the cash flow of the income.

What's the most important factor in determining the value of your home? A realtor would say it's three factors—location, location, and location. The same home, even painted and decorated exactly the same, can bring different prices depending on where you set it down.

You can do your own quick analysis of what your home is worth by finding out what some neighboring properties have sold for. Be sure to adjust their prices, both pluses and minuses, for such factors as differing square footage or different numbers of bathrooms or bedrooms. The most recent sales are usually the best indicator and should always be within the last three months. Anything older than six months should definitely not be included; market values can change quickly.

An example from the authors' personal experience was a lender who tried to make a loan in a very small town in south central Illinois. It was difficult to use the market analysis approach, because there had not been a house sale in this town in the last five years!

Once the appraisal is completed, a value is established for your property. This value is used to determine how much equity you have in your property and how much can be loaned on that property.

Loan-to-Value Ratio

The loan-to-value ratio is a ratio used by lenders to determine the amount of loanable equity in your real estate. In Table 9-1 are shown two

Table 9-1
Example of 75% Loan To Value

Method A		*Method B*	
Value of Property	$100,000	Value of Property	$100,000
LTV Ratio	x 75%	Less First Mortgage	- $50,000
Loanable Amount	$75,000	Equity	$50,000
Less First Mortgage	- $50,000	LTV Ratio	x 75%
Amount of Loan Equity Available	$25,000	Amount of Loan Equity Available	$37,500

examples of a loan-to-value calculation, in both cases using an appraised $100,000 value and a 75 percent loan-to-value ratio. But the ratio is applied at different points in the calculation.

In the first method, the 75 percent loan-to-value (LTV) ratio is applied directly to the appraised value. This leaves a $75,000 loanable amount. After subtracting the first mortgage of $50,000, loan equity available is $25,000. This is the maximum amount a lender will lend you on an equity loan or an equity line of credit.

In the second method, the mortgage is first subtracted from the appraised value for an equity figure of $50,000. Then the LTV is applied for a loan equity available figure of $37,500.

As you can see, the two methods yield quite different amounts. Which method is most frequently used by lenders? Method A gives lenders a greater safety cushion in your property should something happen where they have to repossess and then resell. Therefore, Method A is used most often. By the way, not all lenders use a 75 percent LTV percentage. An LTV of 80 percent is quite common, although going above 80 percent is rarely found.

Can you include the value of an improvement if the funds from the home equity loan are going to be used to improve the house when determining market value? Can the appraisal be adjusted to include the additional square footage of a future bedroom? The answers are "maybe" and "it depends." The improvement to the house can be included in the appraised value if the lender takes some steps to assure that the improvement is actually done, such as not disbursing funds until the improvement is completed or having multiple disbursements as the improvement progresses. Remember, no improvement adds dollar-for-dollar value. So if the cost of the improvement is $20,000, it does not necessarily add $20,000 to the value of the property. Some improvements yield more value than other types, and the actual values of improvements are best left to an appraiser's expert assessment.

You can compute your own maximum loan amount based on the LTV ratio by using Table 9-2. Estimate the value of your home and enter that on line 1. That was simple, wasn't it? Makes you wonder why appraisers get paid so much! Next apply the LTV ratio of 75 percent, or you could use 80 percent as many lenders do. But lenders are more conservative for second mortgages than they are for firsts, so 75 percent

Table 9-2
Computing Your Own Ratio

1.	Estimated Value of Your Home	$______________
2.	LTV Ratio	___________x 75%
3.	Loanable Amount Including First Mortgage	$______________
4.	Subtract First Mortgage	$______________
5.	Maximum Loan Amount	$______________

is becoming more common. Multiply line 1 by line 2 and enter the figure on line 3. This is the loanable amount including any first mortgage. Estimate the balance of your first mortgage based on your last statement and subtract that from line 3. Enter the result on line 5 as the maximum loan amount.

If you already have a second mortgage outstanding, ignore it at this point. Most lenders will require that it be paid off before they will make you an equity loan rather than lending on a third or fourth mortgage. In reality, a second mortgage lender will include the amount of any previously existing second mortgage in the Maximum Loan Amount. The new lender will "take out" the existing second-mortgage lender, meaning that the new loan will include enough to pay off the old second mortgage. Then your new lender will have full rights on your property as the only second-mortgage holder.

How a Lender Looks at You

How do you suppose lenders will look at you when considering whether to make you a loan? Their judgment is strongly influenced by how correct they have to be. If they make a mistake, the property could wind up in foreclosure, which is a very expensive proposition for all parties. So how often can lenders make mistakes and how often do they have to be right? Let's take some examples. If you were in Las Vegas, how often would you have to be right to end up a winner? The answer to that one is fairly easy. If you were right 51 percent of the time and lost only 49 percent of the time, you would come out ahead, even if only a little bit. Let's take another example—flying. The last time you flew in a commercial airliner, what percentage of the time did you want the air traffic controller to be right? Probably 110 percent.

Now the parameters have been set. A loan officer must be right somewhere between 51 percent and 110 percent. To narrow it down, how often can a loan officer afford to be wrong and still have a job? Well, the national loan loss ratio on this type of a loan is a little less than one-half of one percent. Therefore, loan officers have to be right about 99.5 percent of the time. And that's a pretty high percentage. So lenders are going to be very conservative when evaluating your credit.

With this background, let's take a look to see how that magic decision to say yes or no is reached. Assuming you have equity and assuming the loan-to-value ratio that the lender uses will result in the loan amount you want, lenders now must look at your ability to repay the loan. To assist lenders to determine your ability to repay, they have something called the *Five C's of Credit*. No matter how valuable your collateral may be, it is you who make out that payment check each month, not your collateral.

The Five C's Of Credit

Almost all lenders are familiar with three C's of credit. But actually there are five, and loan officers usually learn these at their mother's knee. These C's determine whether you get your loan and for how much. They are Capacity, Character, Collateral, Capital and Conditions.

Capacity

Capacity refers to the ability of the individual to repay a loan. This capacity is normally determined through income levels. Common sources of income would be wages and salaries, commissions, and interest from savings.

Loan officers will count income only if they can verify the amount and that it will continue throughout the term of the loan. Verification of the level of income can be done by a variety of means, such as a letter sent to your employer concerning your income, a tax return, a W-2, or a paystub. When verifying continuation of the income, loan officers want the income to continue at least as long as the loan. So if you apply for a five-year home equity loan, lenders will want to ascertain that your income will continue for five years.

Lenders will add up all your sources of income, weigh the probability that these sources will continue, and see if the result will support the loan payments. They will also often figure out a debt ratio, which is discussed in more detail later in this chapter, to determine if it's within acceptable levels. If the answers to these analyses are acceptable, then capacity has been satisfied. If the answer is no, then you flunk the first test and you will probably be turned down.

Character

Assuming you do have the capacity to repay, will you want to? The willingness to repay the loan revolves around the question of moral character. Some borrowers who just barely have the capacity will qualify because they have excellent character. And others who have excellent capacity won't pay because of poor habits or even criminal intent. Consumers with poor character generally don't get loans because they cause more trouble than they're worth, no matter how high the loan is priced.

Judging character is far more difficult than judging capacity. The most time-honored way is to pull a credit bureau report, which is a listing of all the borrower's past credits. This report lists payment history, so lenders can see how the individual paid other creditors. If other creditors were paid satisfactorily, then it can be assumed that the person applying for the loan will also pay this loan satisfactorily. If problems are noted in a borrower's payment history, then the loan is either rejected or an explanation is requested by the lender. If you know of past credit problems that may show up on your credit report, and if you have an explanation for them, bring them up at the time of application, because lenders will surely find out, and it is far better to offer the explanation up front than to be asked about it later.

Collateral

Collateral is property you own that the lender can use to secure the loan, so if you don't repay, the collateral can be sold to repay the loan. In the case of a home equity loan, the collateral is the equity in your home. This C has been discussed extensively throughout this book and is revisited again in Chapter Twelve.

These three, Capacity, Character, and Collateral, are the basic three C's of credit. But there are two more your lender should consider.

Capital

Capital is an added plus that should not be overlooked. While lenders generally take an income approach to your financial condition, examining the cash inflow versus the cash outflow, the balance sheet is also an important component of credit, and lenders do consider your capital position. We have seen cases where individuals with a net worth or capital position of over $1 million have borrowed only because their accountants have told them to do so for tax purposes. Lenders don't normally overlook a strong capital position. If you have one, be sure to note it somewhere on the application form.

Conditions

The final C has less to do with you yourself than where you are. Certain regions of the country aren't doing as well as others. For example, in late 1987, properties in Boston were appreciating at record levels whereas properties in Houston were not. In fact, properties in Houston were being devalued. If you are unlucky enough to live in a region of the country that is economically depressed, the "conditions" can dampen a lender's enthusiasm no matter what your other qualifications happen to be. In this case, you may be better off finding an out-of-town lender, since local lenders may be reluctant to provide equity loans in such an environment.

These are The Five C's of Credit that constitute the decision-making process for the granting of your loan. However, they still boil down to two key items—the ability to repay and the willingness to repay. If you can demonstrate that you have both of these qualifications, then you should be able to find a home equity loan in the amount you need.

The Debt Ratio

As mentioned previously, to determine capacity loan officers will frequently calculate the debt ratio to help them quantify your ability to repay. Basically, a debt ratio is the percentage of your monthly income that is required to repay all of your outstanding loans, credit card debt, auto loans, and other obligations. Table 9-3 enables you to calculate your own debt ratio.

Table 9-3
Calculating Your Debt Ratio

Step 1: Monthly Payment		**Step 2: Verifiable Gross Monthly Income**	
1st Mortgage	$________	Wages/Salaries 1	$________
Vehicle 1	________	Wages/Salaries 2	________
Vehicle 2	________	Bonus/Commission	________
Credit Cards:		Interest/Dividends	________
________	________	Other	________
________	________	Other	________
________	________		
Loan applied for	________		
Other	________		
Other	________		
Other	________		
Total Monthly Bills	$________	Total Monthly Income	$________

Step 3:

$$\frac{\text{Bills (Step 1)}}{\text{Income (Step 2)}} = \frac{\_\_\_\_\_\_}{} \times 100 = \_\_\_\_\_\_ \text{\% Debt Ratio}$$

First, list the payments for all debts currently outstanding in Step1. In the left hand column list your current monthly payment for your first mortgage, including taxes and insurance. Then list payments for any auto or truck or vehicle loans you may have, including insurance payments, then credit cards, such as Visa, MasterCard, or Sears, and then any other monthly obligations. Don't include normal monthly living expenses like food or clothing. This list will then consist of your ongoing monthly debt obligations. The one other obligation you must include is your anticipated payment on the home equity loan for which you plan on applying. If you are unsure of what this will be, use the Monthly Payment Calculator in the appendix to calculate an estimated payment.

To the right in the table, do Step 2 and list your monthly income. Include wages, salaries, bonuses, commissions, interest, and dividends. Income that is received on a yearly basis should be divided by 12. Keep in mind that lenders must be able to verify all the income you've listed. If you operate a cash business for which you may not report all the income or if you work a second job where you get paid in cash which you may not report, this income cannot be verified in writing, so it won't count as far as a lender is concerned.

Add up the totals to calculate the total monthly payments due and the total monthly income received. Now divide the total monthly bills by the total monthly income and multiply by 100. The result is a percentage called the *gross debt ratio.*

The debt ratio defines the percentage of your gross monthly income required to repay your monthly obligations. This is your cash inflow compared to your cash outflow.

What debt ratios are lenders looking for? The average debt ratio most lenders want is 35 percent to 37 percent. Some lenders will go into the 40 percent area, and other lenders will restrict themselves to 30 percent or 33 percent. The debt ratio lenders are willing to accept depends upon how conservative they are, what quality they want in their loan portfolio, and what your capital position is. The lower the percentage, meaning the higher the income and the lower the bills, the greater the likelihood that this loan will not become a collection item.

Some lenders don't use this ratio. They use other methodologies for determining ability to repay, such as a net debt ratio or some type of scoring system. But this is the ratio used most commonly. If the gross debt ratio is too high, the lender may require that you use the new equity loan to pay off some of these bills. Remember that you always list the loan for which you're applying in the monthly payment column. But if you're going to pay off one of your other obligations with the proceeds of the equity loan, then you don't have to include it in the calculation of the debt ratio, since only those bills remaining after the loan is made are included.

The gross debt ratio is used not only for determining capacity but also for setting the size of the loan you can handle, as discussed next.

Setting the Line Size

One of the restrictions on how large a loan you can obtain is, of course, the amount of equity you have in your home. Another very important restriction is your ability to repay. These two factors must be coordinated to determine the size of the loan you can obtain. You may have $100,000 equity in your home, but your debt ratio may indicate you can only support another $50,000 in debt. Then lenders won't give you more than $50,000. The reverse is also true. If you can support $100,000 in additional debt, but you only have $50,000 equity in your house, lenders will again only give you $50,000. The restriction is the lower of the equity or the debt capacity.

How can you independently calculate the maximum amount you can get? One way is to use the debt ratio. Using Table 9-3, assuming a 37 percent debt ratio, which is a fairly common average for lenders, multiply the total income listed by 37 percent. This amount is the total monthly income available for debt repayments. Now subtract all your monthly payments for the first mortgage, vehicles and credit cards. Do not include any projected payments for a home equity line. The amount left is available for any additional monthly bills, such as for a home equity loan. In order to convert this potential monthly payment to an annual line, go to the appendix. Using some appropriate interest rate, like something a lender has quoted you, and an appropriate term such as ten years, go into the body of the table to find a payment amount. Divide this payment amount into the calculated debt capacity amount. This figure times $1,000 is the line amount you can afford.

Table 9-4 shows an example of this method. Step 1 starts with your gross monthly income and multiplies it times the debt ratio of 37 percent. This results in your gross debt capacity.

Table 9-4
Setting a Line Size

Step 1:	Gross Monthly Income	$2,500.00
	times Debt Ratio (37%)	x .37
	Gross Debt Capacity	$925.00
Step 2:	Gross Debt Capacity	$925.00
	Less: First Mortgage	450.00
	Car	150.00
	Credit Card Payments	60.00
	Available for Second Mortgage	$265.00
Step 3:	Amount Available for Second Mortgage	$265.00
	Divided by Appendix Payment Factor (10% rate for 10 years)	$13.22
	Line Amount Factor	20.045385
	x $1,000	$20,045.39

Affordable line amount at selected rate and term =

$20,045.39

Step 2 subtracts existing debt from the $925 gross debt capacity resulting in $265 being available for new debt, in this case a home equity line of credit.

Step 3 requires you to go to the Monthly Payment Calculator in the appendix. You pick a rate and a term. You can use ten years for an average term, and in this case we will use a rate of ten percent. You would normally use actual rates for your own area.

Using a ten percent rate for ten years results in a payment factor of $13.22 per thousand. Divide $13.22 into the amount you have available for a second mortgage, and you have your line amount factor of

20.045385. Multiply this times $1,000, and you have now calculated your affordable line, which in this example is $20,045.39.

The Importance of Past Payment Habits

The gross debt ratio and the setting of the line amount are used to determine ability to pay. Past payment habits are an essential factor when determining willingness to pay, which is harder to figure out. Has the borrower paid his or her bills in the past? If so, then the probability of prompt payment in the future is better than if payment habits are sloppy. However, is past performance predictive of future performance? Most lenders at least hope that it is because that's how they determine whether or not you have the willingness to repay a loan. They look to see what you did in the past. They assume that good performance in the past will mean good performance in the future and that poor performance in the past will mean poor performance in the future.

Most lenders obtain this knowledge from what's called a credit bureau report. The local credit-reporting agency will have a file on you that lists your various creditors over the past years and how you paid those creditors. There is a fee lenders must pay to get this report, and they usually pass the fee on to you as part of the application fee. One of the things they check in a credit-bureau report is if you've had sufficient credit in the past. If you've never borrowed and have no history, you will have a hard time getting a loan. Also, one department-store account that's been open for six months probably isn't enough of a history to prove whether or not you have the willingness to repay your debts. If you have a limited credit history, the lender must make some kind of judgment based on your employment stability and any additional information you can provide.

The lender can also contact creditors you may have listed on your application form whether or not they were listed in the credit report. Even if they were in the credit bureau report, a lender can get more current information by talking with them directly. You give the lender permission to contact other creditors, usually when you sign the application form but sometimes when you sign a separate permission form, which is in turn mailed to other creditors.

The Results of Poor Credit

If you have had poor credit in the past, getting a home equity loan is more difficult. Especially difficult is to get a loan at a local institution with a reasonable rate. Otherwise, you can contact "lenders of last resort," who for very high rates and with substantial equity will make loans to individuals who have had credit problems in the past. Since the loans that these types of lenders will make are typically riskier and result in more defaults, they charge a higher interest rate and are very careful about assessing the value of the collateral, both of which keep them from absorbing too many losses. These lenders, however, are more likely to foreclose at an early stage rather than work with you on a repayment plan if you get into trouble.

The bottom line is that bad credit makes applying for loans more difficult. If you do have bad credit due to extenuating circumstances, advise lenders of this at application time. Tell them the circumstances. Reasonable lenders consider all the reasons for the bad credit before making a decision. If you're not up front about this problem, lenders may summarily turn down the loan or perhaps come back to you and ask you for that explanation. But they will remember that it was they and not you who had to take that step.

Annual Reviews

Another important step in analyzing the character of your credit is the annual review. Just because you qualified for your home equity loan when you originally applied doesn't mean that a deterioration of your credit standing won't affect this loan. An annual review is when a lender on some periodic basis reunderwrites your loan to see if you are still good for the money. Reviews are generally done on an annual basis. This won't have much effect if you've drawn out your full line, but if any of the line is still unused a lender can restrict its future access to you.

Some lenders may require additional information or a personal financial statement, while other lenders will only recheck your credit bureau status for any adverse trends or reportings. Lenders' approach to a review is to determine in their own mind if they would approve your loan again based on the updated information. The answer is normally yes, but if it is no, then your lender will probably restrict you from making further draws. If this happens to you, keep in mind that your lender must notify you in writing that the account is restricted.

What to Do if the Loan Is Denied

Even if you're absolutely sure you've got great credit, you're still going to worry a little about what will happen if you're turned down. One of the ways to alleviate that fear is to know ahead of time what will happen.

Lenders' Responsibilities

If your loan is denied, Federal regulations require the lender to notify you in writing of the denial and the reasons for the denial. This is called an *adverse action notice.* If some significant portion of the request is changed—for example, if you requested a $40,000 line of credit and the lender only approved $30,000—they would be required to send you the same adverse-action notice that the loan request was modified.

If the reason for the denial was based on credit information from some source other than the lender, they must also disclose what that source is. The source may have been some other creditor who gave you a bad credit rating or perhaps a credit bureau report that listed some bad credit ratings. In any case, the lender must do more than just call you up and say that your loan is not approved. The lender must, according to regulation, send you in writing the reasons why your loan was not approved.

Credit Bureau Responsibilities

If your loan is denied or modified because of information obtained in a credit-bureau report, you have certain rights pertaining to this credit bureau reporting agency. If you provide the agency with a copy of your adverse-action notice showing that your loan was denied based on the information received from their agency, you may request a free copy of the report. Of course, you can at any time obtain a copy of your own credit report, but normally you would have to pay a fee for this service. If you are denied credit, this service is free. Then you have the right to sit down with representatives of the credit bureau and discuss the report and the facts contained within the report. If you feel these facts are incorrect, you may dispute the facts in writing. The credit bureau then will contact the creditor involved that gave the questionable credit information and ask for verification. If the creditor does not respond within a certain period of time, then the credit bureau must, by law, remove the adverse rating from their file.

You also have the right, again at no charge, to place your own statement of explanation within the credit bureau file. If the rating is, in fact, correct and you know it to be correct, but you want to tell your side of the story, then you have a right to have a statement placed in the file. Every time a creditor prints out your credit-bureau file, your statement is included along with the original report.

You have a right to take these actions under the law. There's not a thing wrong with you using those rights, and we encourage you to do so as needed.

What Lenders *Really* Look for

A lot of credit criteria have been covered in this chapter. Collateral, the equity contained in that collateral, and how that equity is calculated were all discussed. Then the criteria for evaluating you as a borrower were examined, and we explained how you stack up as far as the lender is concerned. But when all is said and done, what is it that lenders *really* look for? That depends on which of the two basic types of equity lenders in the market today you're dealing with. The first type has a focus on collateral, and the second type has a focus on the applicant.

Collateral Focus

The collateral-focused lender is really more interested in the collateral than in the person who's applying for the credit. These lenders will look very, very closely at the value of the property. And as long as you as the borrower are breathing, they're satisfied. If you have a really poor credit history, they may turn you down, but as long as you meet the collateral requirements and the debt-ratio requirements are somewhere in the range of 37 percent, these types of lenders will usually approve the loan.

Applicant Focus

The lender who is focused on the applicant also wants to make sure the collateral has the value needed and that it is appraised properly, but these types of lenders are really more interested in the applicant and his or her ability and willingness to repay. These lenders will be more critical of past credit problems than the collateral-focused lenders.

Which to Choose

The type of lender you choose will of course be up to you, but initially it is just luck which kind you get, since you won't know until your application is being processed which type you're dealing with. Some lenders are well balanced between the two, but usually lenders tend toward one focus or the other. The easiest lender to deal with in general is probably the one you've done business with in the past. You know each other, and from your past dealings together this lender already knows your willingness to repay the loan. All they will have to do is to update the information to determine if you still have debt capacity to repay a new loan and that the collateral meets the lender's own requirements.

Strategies

This is the mystical art of lending in a nutshell. Although it takes a lot of analysis and years of experience to make the right choices and decisions, a lot of it is common sense. Although the application process can get pretty frustrating at times, just remember that the lender on the other side of the desk has to beat those 99.5 percent odds. So help lenders out and give them all the information you can. That will make their job easier and will get your loan approved faster.

Over the years we have made more loans than we want to remember, but occasionally even the experts can make a mistake. If you are denied credit, there are some things we think you can do. First, you need to know the reason. Many times there are alternatives.

If you were denied because of insufficient equity, then the appraisal may have been lower than you thought. You can request a copy of the appraisal or at least ask to know what the value of your house was judged to be. Different lenders usually use different appraisers and, since appraising is not an exact science, it is possible to reapply and be approved by another lender. You may even get your own appraisal, at a cost, of course, and then find out what factor or combination of factors is making the property value lower than anticipated; perhaps these could be changed.

If the question is an ability to repay, you can work with your lender to look at consolidating some bills into your equity loan, thus making the loan more affordable to you in the lender's eyes. It is perfectly acceptable to ask lenders how they calculate an ability to repay. Again, different lenders have different requirements, and you may be approved by one or another lender.

Chapter Ten

Shopping for a Home Equity Loan

Home equity loans are like those little cars seen all over the roads these days. It seems like everybody is selling them. In any major metropolitan market, it's hard to open the business section of a newspaper or the home section of a Sunday paper without being barraged by ads for home equity loans. And if that isn't enough, lenders are even sending you mail offers for home equity loans. So it's an important point to make that this is a market not controlled by the lenders. It is controlled by *you,* meaning you can be choosey and wait to find thc loan that is just right for you. It almost seems as if there are more lenders out there seeking your business than there are consumers wanting to take out these loans, so somewhere you can find the institution that has a loan with the features that will work just right for you.

Before you begin shopping, keep in mind that you don't really want a home equity loan. This seemingly strange attitude can save you a lot of time and money. Never forget what it is you really want. You don't want a loan; you want what that loan will buy. So if the loan is not structured to suit your needs to allow you to buy what it is you want, whether a new addition or a better education for your child, then just walk away. Remember, consumers vote with their feet. So find a lender who will meet your needs, give you the loan you want, and furnish a level of service that will make it easy for you not only to obtain the loan but also to service the loan throughout its life.

Who Offers These Loans?

Home equity loans and home equity lines of credit are offered by a variety of lenders. The most familiar are the banks, savings and loans, finance companies, and credit unions, but they are not the only ones that offer this product. Both banks and savings and loans are about equally likely to offer this loan. Only about a third of them do not offer some type of an equity loan. Some may offer only the closed end and not the open end, but almost two-thirds offer some type of home equity loan. So both banks and savings and loans can be prime candidates for a place to shop for this product.

Credit unions also offer this product. Especially the larger ones have recently been offering home equity loan products. If you are a member of a credit union now, ask if they offer this product, because the cost structures and expense structures of a credit union are often lower than that of banks and savings and loans, and some of them offer real bargains.

Finance companies have been offering equity loans for years. The days are gone where the finance companies specialize in small personal loans of $200 or $300. Most of the finance companies now are offering larger loans and especially second mortgages. While finance company loans are not always the lowest priced on the market, many times they are the easiest to obtain. This end of the financial industry learned many years ago to provide a product without intimidation. They've traded in their three-piece suits and replaced them with a hearty handshake and a smile, so their image is just regular folks. Some of these companies will offer the loans by mail or phone as well as making it especially easy for you to apply.

Entering the market these days are a number of institutions often called non-banks, such as the Sears Financial Network. Also, financial companies like Shearson/American Express have offered this product for a number of years through their money management type of accounts. While these companies do not have a particularly large market share, it is worthwhile to know that they are in the market, and they occassionally offer very competitive pricing.

Another new entry into the market is General Motors. Through their finance subsidiary, General Motors Acceptance Corporation (GMAC), they offer first mortgages as well as second mortgages. The second mortgage program is being offered in limited market areas, but it is reasonable to assume that GMAC, which is a powerful force in the marketplace, can be expected to expand in the future.

What to Look for

What to look for in a second mortgage loan is not quite as simple as what to look for in buying a home initially. When purchasing a house, the three critical factors are location, location, and location! With a home equity loan, the four elements you need to consider when selecting a lender are:

(1) Service
(2) Location
(3) Price
(4) Knowledge of product

Service

Service is perhaps most important. Home equity loans are generally priced competitively, so service becomes more important than price. The old saying is true that you pay for what you get or don't get, meaning that what you gain in price you may give up in service. Both when you first obtain the loan and later when the loan has to be serviced, service is very important and valuable, so it is worth your while to spend a little more for good service.

How do you know whether an institution will give you good service if you've never dealt with them before? First, start with your current bank, savings and loan, or credit union. You know the quality of their service and whether you would want a home equity loan from them based upon your experience. Evaluating new institutions is a bit harder. Talk to them on the phone. How is your request handled? Do they know the answers to your questions? Is the literature you ask for sent out promptly and is it complete? The initial impressions you get of an institution are a good indication of future service. If you're not properly handled when you ask about a product, then chances are you won't be properly handled when you need service on that product.

Location

Location may or may not be important to you. A national survey, done by Moebs $ervices and Market Facts in mid-1986* found that 83

* *Home Equity Lines II*, Market Facts, Inc., Chicago, and Moebs $ervices, Wadsworth, Illinois (1987).

percent of all current home equity line of credit borrowers and 78 percent of all current closed end loan borrowers did use a local lender. Although it may not matter that your credit card is serviced out of South Dakota or Florida, a second mortgage on your house may be better gotten with a lender that is a little closer. There is some comfort in being able to walk in and talk to a real person face to face versus a computer or someone a thousand miles away over the phone. This doesn't mean a loan can't be serviced just as well by a non-local service center. On the contrary, there are some companies that provide excellent service despite the fact that they are many miles away. Nonetheless, location is an important consideration for many borrowers.

Price

Price should be one of the primary factors. Although a loan shouldn't be totally price-driven, there is a limit as to how much any credit product or any feature of a credit product is worth. The breakeven point, that point where you are indifferent whether you get the loan or not, is where the marginal cost of credit is less than the marginal utility you will derive from its use. Any product, no matter how well it is designed, can still be rejected on the basis that it is really not worth the price. So when you're shopping, keep price in mind. You can get the price from advertisements that you see in newspapers, your mail, television, or hear from radio. These will give you a good feel for the rates, terms, and various types of programs being offered within your area. Remember that many lenders will meet the best deal but not necessarily advertise it. So always try to get the best price.

Knowledge of Product

When you call an institution to get some information about an equity loan, you should note carefully how well they answer your questions and know the product. This can be a complicated loan. If all you want is rate information, the receptionist who answers the phone can probably give you that. But if you aren't that knowledgeable about financial products and you want some guidance and detailed explanations, you will probably be transferred to a loan officer. This person should then be able to answer all your questions without any problem. You should be very hesitant about taking out an equity loan with a lender who doesn't seem to know what it is or how it works. If they don't know and you don't know (that's why you're asking them questions), both of you are liable to have some nasty surprises somewhere down the line. The less you know, the more your lender should know and be willing to share with you.

In summary, price is a big factor for an equity loan. But equally as important is service and the lender's knowledge of and willingness to stand behind the product. And there is always the convenience of having a lender close by. These four factors should be weighed together. You will probably find that trade-offs have to be made. Know what is important to you, and don't sacrifice the one factor that is very important to you for another factor that may not really matter.

Using Your Existing Mortgage Lender

Certainly the most convenient option is for you to use the institution that holds your current first mortgage. If you've had past problems with them and object to their service, then you are just asking for more trouble if you decide to do additional business with them. But if your relationship with this lender is satisfactory, then there is no reason why you shouldn't use them, or at least take a look at their equity loan program.

There are several advantages of using your first mortgage lender. First, they know who you are, they've done business with you for a number of years, they've already approved you for a substantial amount of credit, and you have a good track record with them. Second, they know your house because they've already made a loan on that property. Because of these reasons, they may be more willing than others to make you the second mortgage loan. There's a lot of flexibility in this arrangement because you both know each other. So we recommend that unless you have had some real problems with them in the past, your first mortgage lender should at least be considered as a source for a home equity loan.

There are, however, some disadvantages. Some lenders don't like to see second mortgages when they already have the first mortgage. The collateral on which they initially lent, the house, is being too highly leveraged, which they may feel puts their first mortgage in jeopardy. In fact, some loan agreements for first mortgages prohibit second mortgages. If your current lender has that covenant in the mortgage agreement, then you can't use this lender for an equity loan and may not be able to get a second mortgage from any lender. A second consideration is service. If the service from your current lender has been unsatisfactory in the past, you're asking for trouble to use them for a second loan. Whatever your relationship with your current mortgage lender, you should at least include them in your initial investigation. The advantages may outweigh the disadvantages.

Understanding Ads

A quick mention needs to be made about newspaper ads, because many consumers use home equity loan ads as their main source to comparison shop. In fact, according to the Moebs $ervices/Market Facts study,* between 13 percent and 28 percent of consumers learned about their current home equity loan from ads. Many lenders find that ads are the most effective means for advertising to potential users of the home equity loan. And reading ads in newspapers gives consumers a good general sense of the market to see who is aggressive in equity lending.

Another type of advertising is direct mail. Fully 40 percent of line of credit users and 21 percent of closed end loan users learned about their loan through direct mail. The points made below about advertising apply to direct mail ads as well as newspaper ads.

You will find that advertising tends to follow two patterns. One is those lenders who advertise only one thing—price. These lenders offer either the lowest price in town or a loan with very few up-front fees. Although a good price is important, the other three factors of service, location, and knowledge also matter. Don't just go for price with an institution that won't stand behind its loan or service it properly. While there is nothing wrong with considering lenders who advertise only price, you would want to examine such a lender carefully. When lenders cut price, they also have to cut the level of service, or they lose money. Losing money is not the favorite sport of lenders, so look closely at their

* op. cit.

service. These lenders may take much longer to approve your application, or they may not approve it at all. A lower price could mean the lender will be very particular about whom they will approve, such as only higher-equity individuals or high-wealth applicants.

As you look at newspaper ads, look at what the institution is offering besides price. Be sure to read the fine print. There you can often find out what other fees will be charged. This allows you to compare loans accurately, because although the rate may be very low, you might have a lot of up-front fees which will ultimately make the loan very expensive. It doesn't do you much good to get what you consider to be a very good up-front rate but then be burdened down with high fees. So the smaller the print in the ad, the kind you have to use a magnifying glass to read, the more important it is that you read it.

Comparison Shopping

Putting all the features together that were discussed in Chapters Six, Seven, and Eight can seem to be a mammoth job. Actually it's not so bad. To assist you in comparing lenders, which in the trade is called *comparison shopping*, tables are included in this chapter for variable rate closed end loans, fixed rate closed end loans, and open end lines of credit.

Variable Rate Closed End Home Equity Loan

Table 10-1 lists all the questions you should ask for a variable rate closed end loan and gives a framework for exactly how to compare lenders. The questions you get to ask on the phone when you do comparison shopping is the fun part. Call some lenders, compare their prices, and ask those pointed questions, so that you can choose which equity loan is best for you. You can make a chart just like Table 10-1 when you do your own shopping around. The table assumes there are three lenders called; you may have more.

Interest Rate. First ask about interest rate and the features having to do with rate. Since this is a variable rate loan, ask about today's rate. Then ask about the index, the spread over the index, the cap, the floor, and how

Table 10-1
Comparison between
Variable Rate Closed End Loans
$20,000 Loan

	Lender A	*Lender B*	*Lender C*
Interest Rate			
Rate—Variable	10.75%	10.25%	10.50%
Index	3-month T-bill	Prime Rate	FHLBB Cost of Funds
Spread	+ 4.50%	+ 3.00%	+ 2.50%
APR	10.75%	10.91%	10.87%
Cap	6.00%	6.00%	6.00%
Floor	5.00%	3.00%	5.00%
Adjustment Frequency	Quarterly	Quarterly	Annually
Fees			
Application Fee	$0	$125	$50
Points	0.00%	1.50%	1.50%
Closing Costs	$300	$325	$0
Other			
Term	120 mos	60 mos	120 mos
Prepayment Penalty	No	No	No
Payment	$272.68	$427.41	$269.87
Service			
Brochures	Yes	Yes	Yes
Application Kit	No	Yes	No
How Long to Approve	2 weeks	4 weeks	1 week
Service Location	Local	Out of State	Local
How Long to Receive Info	7 days	10 days	8 days

often the rate is adjusted. Note especially the rate; this is the index plus the spread on an example day. If you were to select a lender on rate alone, you would select the lowest rate, which is Lender B.

Fees. But you don't want to consider only rate. Look at the next group—fees. Remember there is an offset between fees and rate. What you really want is the APR. Ask about points, application fee and closing costs. Points have to be included in the APR, so ask what those fees are.

When you ask about fees, you should tell the lender how much you want to borrow and what you plan to use the money for. There are lenders who will vary the cost by the product type. For example, borrowing for home improvement may well be less expensive than borrowing for bill consolidation. Studies have shown that the purpose of the loan does have an effect on the risk and, thus, the price. Home improvement is the lowest risk of these loan types, whereas consolidation and investments are among the highest of the risk types. So be sure to disclose the purpose of the loan. Also, sometimes an application fee is refundable. You may be willing to pay a higher application fee if you know you'll get it back. Lender A has no application fee, Lender B has a $125 fee, and Lender C charges only $50. So Lender A would be the cheapest whereas Lender B is more than twice as high as Lender C. You should ask if the application fee is refundable.

Term / Payment. You can then ask about other features, such as term. Shorter terms will increase your monthly payments and also increase the yield to the lender and, therefore, increase the cost of credit to you. This is because fees figured as a percentage of the total balance over a shorter period of time increases the yield due to the present value of money. Therefore, the shorter the term is, the lower the fees should be.

Considering term as well as rate, Lender C has the lowest payment and therefore is the most attractive to you from a budget standpoint. Lender A comes in second. And Lender B has the highest payment, but this is due largely to the shorter term. For a real comparison, the terms should be reviewed on a uniform basis.

Service. Service, while important, is last on your comparison shopping list, because questions having to do with service are often not answered over the phone. First ask whether the lender has brochures and if they can be mailed to you. Then ask whether they have an application kit. If you are really interested in their program and they have a kit, go ahead and ask for it. An application kit makes it much easier to apply for the loan and allows you to fill out many of the forms in the comfort of your own home rather than going into the lender's institution. You also want to know how long it'll take to approve the loan. The lender should be able to give you a ballpark figure.

How far are you willing to go for service? Ask about the location of a service facility where you can ask questions about a billing problem or a missing payment. If the lender is local, you should rate that relatively high because of the convenience involved. Finally, how long did it take to receive the information that you requested? If you have to make a follow-up call to get it, that doesn't speak well for the service level of the institution. Different departments within an institution tend to have the same level of service, so the people who are supposed to send you information will usually give you the same type of service you will find in the loan area. Service tends to be mainly a function of management perspective than individual efforts, and it is up to management to place emphasis on providing a good level of service. How long it takes to get information and the quality of what you're sent says a lot about the institution.

Time To Choose. Let's take a look at this variable rate closed end loan. You've gathered all the data you can. Now which one would you choose? Lender A has the lowest APR, but if you choose that one you are wrong! Remember our discussion in Chapter Seven about rates and fees. Well, how about Lender B? It has the lowest rate. Wrong again. From a cost standpoint, Lender C is best,and here's why.

	Lender A	*Lender B*	*Lender C*
Rate	10.75%	10.25%	10.50%
Interest	$12,721	$5,644	$12,384
Up-front fees	0	425	250
Closing fees	300	325	0
Total costs	$13,021	$6,394	$12,634
APR	10.75%	10.91%	10.87%

The APR for Lender C is a bit higher because the 1.5 percent service charge is included in the APR calculation whereas Lender A doesn't include its $300 closing fee in the APR. Remember, closing fees don't have to be part of the APR. If closing fees were to be included, then the cost of your credit, the APR, for Lender A would be 11.12 percent whereas Lender C with all fees would be 10.93 percent.

Lender B is not considered less costly because of the higher fees. The total cost for Lender B is lower only because the term is 60 months rather than 120 months like Lenders A and C. If all fees were included, such as closing costs and application fee, the APR would be 11.92 percent. If you can afford the higher payments for a 60-month term, then you're better off getting your 60-month loan with Lender C.

Now, price is not the only issue, so look at the other factors. Lender C adjusts the payment annually, which means more stability for you. The "other" terms are about even, so there is no issue there. And from a service standpoint, Lender C wins again. It's local and can approve your loan in one week.

So unless your father-in-law owns the institution identified as Lender A or Lender B, your best bet is to go with Lender C. On second thought, the heck with your father-in-law. Go with Lender C anyway. After all, whose loan is this?

Finally, ask about closing costs. These can be considerable and can include appraisal, title, recording, credit, and general fees, as mentioned in Chapter Seven. Lender A has $300 closing costs, Lender B has $325 closing costs, and Lender C has no separate closing costs, because they are included in the $300 service charge. So the APR for Lender C includes all its costs.

Fixed Rate Closed End Home Equity Loan

Table 10-2 presents the features for a closed end home equity loan with a fixed rate. It is the same list as Table 10-1 except that variable rate items such as index, spread, cap, floor, and rate adjustment frequency are omitted, so the list is shorter. You still must, however, consider costs such as points, application fees, closing costs and service items.

You will notice immediately that the fixed rate loans have a higher rate than the variable rate loans. Remember the prior discussions? With

Table 10-2
Comparison between
Fixed Rate Closed End Loans
$20,000 Loan

	Lender A	*Lender B*	*Lender C*
Rate/Interest			
Rate Fixed	12.50%	12.00%	12.50%
Fees			
Application Fee	$0	$125	$250
Points	0.00%	1.50%	0.00%
APR	12.50%	12.67%	12.50%
Closing Costs	$300	$325	$0
Other			
Term	120 mos	60 mos	120 mos
Prepayment Penalty	No	No	No
Payment	$272.68	$427.41	$269.87
Service			
Brochures	Yes	Yes	Yes
Application Kit	No	Yes	No
How Long to Approve	2 weeks	4 weeks	1 week
Service Location	Local	Out of State	Local
How Long to Receive Info	5 days	10 days	7 days

a fixed rate, the lender assumes all of the interest rate risk, so the institution will have to charge a higher price or rate in order to cover that additional risk.

In this example, as with Table 10-1, Lender C offers the best loan. Again, the rate appears higher, but you must also consider the other costs which effectively raise the cost of the loan.

	Lender A	*Lender B*	*Lender C*
Rate	12.50%	12.00%	12.50%
APR	12.50	12.54	12.50
APR with closing cost and application fee	12.88	13.70	12.82

Which lender looks better in a newspaper ad? Why, Lender B, of course, because of the lower rate. But if you read the fine print, you will see that's the more expensive loan. The only risk of choosing Lender C is if the application fee is non-refundable. Then you would lose $250 if you do not take the loan.

Open End Home Equity Line of Credit

The questions dealing with a home equity line of credit listed in Table 10-3 are, on the whole, quite different from the questions that were considered for closed end loans.

The questions dealing with rate are the same as for the variable rate closed end loan except for the question about tiering. Tiering is a unique problem when shopping for an open end home equity loan because the balance can change so often. The nature of this product is for you to draw funds, repay, and then draw funds again. Lenders, in their desire for you to keep a high loan balance with them, "reward" you by offering a better rate for the higher balances. If the lender states that the rate today is 10.5 percent and then also informs you that they have tiering, get out a full-size, blank sheet of paper. You will need a lot of room to record what the tiers are, because the lender will always give you the lowest rate up front, meaning the highest tier, and then you need to also consider all the other possible tiers. The 10.5 percent may only apply to balances above $50,000. Balances below $50,000 may well have rates of 11 percent or even 11.5 percent. So it is important to find out whether an institution has tiers and what those tiers are. Also find out whether the tiers are progressive or non-progressive. The difference between the two is explained in Chapter Five.

It appears that Lender B has the lowest APR, but again add in the value of those costs that you must pay but which are not part of the APR, such as annual fee and closing costs.

Table 10-3
Comparison between
Open End Home Equity Lines Of Credit
$20,000 Line

	Lender A	*Lender B*	*Lender C*
Interest Rate			
Rate Today	11.00%	10.50%	11.50%
Index	Prime	Prime	3-Month T-bill
Spread	2.00%	1.50%	4.50%
APR	11.0%	10.72%	11.50%
Tiering	No	Yes	No
Cap	5.00%	6.00%	6.00%
Floor	5.00%	5.00%	None
Adjustment Frequency	Monthly	With Index	Quarterly
Fees			
Application Fee	$0	$50	$200
Points	0.00%	1.00%	0.00%
Closing Costs	$350	$175	$150
Annual Fee	$20	$25	$0
Other			
Term	120 mos	120 mos	180 mos
Option at End	Refinance	Roll/Refinance	Pay
Minimum Draw	$500	$1,000	None
Access Device	Check	Check	Check
Repayment Method	1.5% prin. + int	1.5% of balance	Interest only
Payment Now	$483.33	$300.00	$191.67
Payment Highest	$566.67	$300.00	$291.67
Service			
Brochures	Yes	Yes	Yes
Application Kit	Yes	Yes	No
How Long to Approve	3-4 weeks	3-4 weeks	2-3 weeks
Service Location	Local	Out of State	Local
How Long to Receive Info	3 days	6 days	5 days

	Lender A	*Lender B*	*Lender C*
APR	11.00%	10.72%	11.50%
APR plus other costs	11.40	11.14	11.75

Here, Lender B is clearly the winner on an APR basis. Lender A has an 11 percent rate today. The index is prime with a two percent spread, meaning your rate is prime plus two percent. The rate has a five percent cap and a five percent floor, so the rate can never go higher than 16.0 percent nor lower than six percent. Lender B has a 10.5 percent rate tied to prime with a spread of 1.5 percent. They do have tiering so you need to find out which tiers have which rates. The cap is six percent with a floor of five percent, and the rate changes when and if the index changes. Lender C has a higher rate, uses the T-bill rate as the index with a spread of 4.5 percent above the T-bill, does not have tiering, has a six percent cap and no floor, and the rate can change quarterly. Also, Lender C is quoting for 15 years, not ten, so if you change the term to ten years, the full cost APR increases from 11.75 percent to 11.80 percent.

Lender A's rate is tied to prime and is subject to change monthly, and Lender B's rate is tied to prime and changes when prime changes. But Lender C's rate is tied to the T-bill rate and can change quarterly. How do these indexes and adjustment frequencies compare? T-bill rates do change quite often even though the changes are slight; therefore, you can count on having a payment change every quarter. Prime doesn't change that often, so your rate may not change monthly (even though it could). So which one is better? It would depend on whether you were in an increasing rate environment or a declining rate environment. In general, from a consumer's standpoint, the prime rate is a better index because it has less volatility.

The fee questions are basically the same questions asked for the two closed end loans. Points will usually be as a percentage of the total line granted rather than the balance outstanding at any point in time.

An additional fee unique to lines of credit is the annual fee. Sometimes annual fees are waived the first year and are only assessed the second year, but even a $20 annual fee can add up to $200 over the life of the loan.

Other items unique to an open end loan include the option at the end of the term. What happens when the loan matures at the end of 120 months or 180 months? As shown, Lender A will refinance the loan for you, Lender B will either roll over the line or refinance it, but Lender C doesn't promise you anything except that it will require that the line be paid off. This is probably negotiable at the time the loan matures.

The minimum draw for Lender A is $500, Lender B allows only draws of at least $1,000, but Lender C has no minimum draw. So if accessibility to your line for a small amount is important to you, then Lender C would be of interest. Also, method of access may be important, but all three are the same in allowing you to use checks.

Repayment minimum differs among the three lenders. Lender A requires 1.5 percent of the principal plus the interest outstanding. Lender B requires 1.5 percent of the principal and interest, or 1.5 percent of the balance. And Lender C requires interest only. The best way to compare these three different payments is to figure out what the payment amount would be. So ask for two payment amounts. First, what would the payment amount be now based on today's rate if you were to take out the entire line? And second, what would the payment amount be at the highest rate allowable by the cap? Based on a $20,000 line, Lender A would have a current payment amount of $483.33. This payment consists of 1.5 percent times $20,000, which is $300, plus all of the interest that is due. And when the rate goes up to the highest level that it can, based on the cap, the lender could charge 16 percent. This rate level would mean that your payment amount could go up to $566.67. Make sure that you can afford such a high payment if you should decide Lender A is the one for you. The payments for Lender B are limited to the amount of principal outstanding, so rising interest rates have no impact on payment amount. In this case, your payments for Lender B would be $300. For Lender C, the payment will vary with the interest rate since it is an interest-only payment.

This payment of $300 minimum for the entire $20,000 line as offered by Lender B may seem very nice. But will $300 pay off the line in 120 months? No, it won't. If you pay only $300 a month after borrowing $20,000, at the end of 120 months or ten years, you will still have $17,000 remaining in your principal. You need to remember this before you let yourself get talked into a low monthly payment. Also, with Lender C you pay interest only, so the full $20,000 is remaining.

The service items are the same as in the closed end loans. Again, keep in mind that the way your request for information is handled is a good indication of how the institution will treat you as a customer. If they fail the test of providing you with brochures in a timely manner, imagine what they could do to your entire loan application.

Strategies

With the help of these comparison charts, shopping for your home equity loan can be a fun experience instead of a gut-wrenching horror! Don't just consider price. Be sure to add in fees when you are considering price. And give service its proper due. If you do your shopping carefully and take your time, you should be able to find the equity loan that is just right for you.

With equity lines of credit, be sure you know what will happen at the end of the term. This is especially true with loans having interest-only repayments.

The comparisons we have made here can be difficult for you to duplicate because closing costs can have a considerable impact on the true cost of your loan, and lenders don't have to include closing costs in the APR. Your lender may legitimately not be able to include them for you, because they need a sophisticated computer program to do so. We suggest that you add up the dollar amounts of all costs and then compare those. Although this will not take into consideration the time value of money, the relative figures will be comparable.

Chapter Eleven

What to Expect at Your Loan Closing

Most people don't like loan closings. You have to take time off from work to go some place that is convenient only to the lender to sign all sorts of documents that make no sense. And then the crowning touch is when the lender tells you how much money you have to pay back over a long period of time, which is enough to scare anyone.

Unfortunately, it's something you have to go through. And not only is it inevitable, it's also very important. This is not a credit card; it's a substantial amount of money secured by your primary asset, your home. So it's important that you know what happens at the loan closing. It will help if you know what forms to expect and what they mean, and that's what this chapter is all about.

The first signal you have that a closing is imminent is when you're notified by the lender that your loan is approved and everything is set for closing on a certain date. At the closing you are handed somewhere between four to nine forms with print that is very, very small. The closer, who is either a lawyer representing the financial institution or a professional closer from the closing company, tells you to sign them but to be sure to read them before you sign them and make sure you understand every term and clause. Of course, a roomful of lawyers took three months to draw up all those forms, but you are expected to read and understand them in less than an hour.

One way to help yourself is to request from the lender (and it's a perfectly legitimate request) that all the closing documents be sent to you in blank. They don't have to be filled in, and many times they're not prepared until just prior to the closing anyway. But go ahead and request the blank documents. Then you'll have an opportunity to go through the documents prior to the loan closing itself. In this way you can ask some questions before closing, when you have more time and don't have the pressure of lawyers sitting there waiting.

Will you need a lawyer at a loan closing on a second mortgage? That depends on whom you ask—us or your attorney. It certainly doesn't hurt to have an attorney involved at some point. If you can get the documents ahead of time, you can send them to your attorney for review. In general, we've seen very few attorneys attend second mortgage or equity loan closings. If your equity loan is for less than $25,000, you probably don't need an attorney. But if you're getting an equity loan for $100,000, you will probably want the safety of more careful legal advice. The choice, however, is up to you; you don't have to have one. And, of course, the need for an attorney has to be balanced against the amount that you're borrowing and the amount that the attorney is going to charge you to show up at the closing.

Important Forms You'll See *before* the Closing

The closing is simply when you actually sign the documents, so that you and the lender have a valid contract. Listed here are the main documents you'll encounter, the purpose of the document, and some highlights of things you should know about each document. Most of these documents are required by the Federal government.

But before you get to the closing, you have already signed some forms and received some forms from the lender. These documents are often included in the package reviewed at closing, and they include the application, the good-faith estimate, an adverse-action form in case your loan request has been altered, and a commitment letter.

The Application

The very first form you sign for a lender is, of course, the application for credit. Its purpose is to provide the lender with the information necessary to make a sound credit decision. It also constitutes a formal request for the product by you, the applicant. The application provides the lender with your approval to run a check on your credit and request a credit bureau report. Once you fill out the application, you generally never see it again; the lender keeps it.

The Good-Faith Estimate

The good-faith estimate, also called the initial disclosure, discloses the payment terms and rates based on prevailing rates at the time of the application as well as the index used and a history of the index. It is normally used with variable rate loans, and it provides you with a sample of how the loan would work under different rate scenarios. You will receive this document signed by the lender either at the time of application or shortly thereafter. There is no need for you to sign this document.

The Adverse-Action Form

This form, which is signed by the lender, advises you that your loan is turned down or that the lender has changed some of the terms of the loan request. You must be notified of either case in writing through an adverse-action form as stipulated by the Federal government. You will receive the original of this form and need not sign it or return it.

The Commitment Letter

The commitment letter *commits* the lender to making the loan based on certain stipulated conditions. If you fulfill those conditions, the lender can't withdraw its promise to make you the loan. The letter should clearly explain the financial terms of the loan and any conditions to its approval. For example, the commitment letter may state the loan is approved subject to your providing to the lender a paid current hazard insurance policy showing the lender as loss payee.

The letter should normally contain the following items:

1. The amount of credit granted; if it's an equity line of credit, the amount of the credit line.
2. The interest rate if fixed.
3. If the rate is variable, the index, the spread, and the frequency of rate change and payment adjustment.
4. The term of the loan.
5. Minimum monthly payment.
6. Fees and closing costs.
7. Access method for an equity line of credit.
8. The date the commitment expires.

9. Any "subject to's" or conditions of approval that you have to fulfill before closing.

You will normally receive the original. Some lenders include an additional copy and ask for you to sign and return the letter. The letter commits the lender but not you unless you sign and return a copy of it. The commitment letter is the offer, and the acceptance is either the customer signing the commitment letter or, more commonly, signing the note.

Important Forms You'll See *at* the Closing

The forms that you may see for the first time at the closing include the right of rescission, the note, the agreement, the truth-in-lending disclosure, the mortgage, the billing-rights statement, and various riders that can occasionally be used.

The Right of Rescission

The right of rescission allows the borrower three full business days to cancel or rescind the transaction. This is also called the cooling-off period. The purpose of the right of rescission is to prevent an unscrupulous lender from talking consumers into taking out second mortgages when they may not really want to. You, therefore, have three days in which to cancel the transaction and back out of the loan. A lien cannot be taken out on your house until the three days expire, but you will also not get the money. The net effect is that this document delays the disbursement of funds to you or the availability of any credit line for three days. You will normally sign this on the closing day and receive your money three days later. All obligated borrowers must sign and will receive their own copy of the form.

The Note

The note is your promise to repay the loan. The note is signed by both you and the lender, and it specifies that you, as a borrower, do promise to repay the loan and stipulates the method of those repayments.

It is one of the few straightforward documents you will sign at the closing. You will, of course, receive your own copy of this document, but the lender holds the original.

The Agreement

Although the note is your promise to pay, the actual terms and conditions of the loan are laid out in the agreement, a much more complicated document. It is signed by both you and the lender and binds both of you to all of the terms of the loan. This is key, that not only are you now bound to the terms and conditions of the loan, but so is the lender. While the lender normally retains the original, you will receive a copy of this document for your files.

You would normally find the following items in an agreement:

1. The date of the agreement.
2. The amount of the line of credit.
3. The term of the loan and what happens upon expiration. If the loan has no set term, then that should be so stated.
4. A reference that this agreement is secured and reference to a mortgage document.
5. The finance charge amount, the spread, the index and the calculation method of the finance charge.
6. The monthly payment, calculation method, the minimum due and when payments are due.
7. Late charge, the method of computation and when assessed.
8. Details of loan fees and charges.
9. Method for cancellation of the loan.
10. A reference to the mortgage if default provisions are detailed. In other words, it is the mortgage that lays out actions that can be taken, such as foreclosure, if you don't pay. Thus, the agreement will refer to the mortgage when specifying these provisions.
11. The method of application of payments, i.e., is the interest or the principal reduced first, and how are miscellaneous amounts such as annual fees, late charges, or insurance charges applied.
12. The right to conduct an annual review and credit check.
13. The right to close your line based on negative results from an annual review.

14. Minimum-draw requirements.
15. Stop-payment procedures if your equity line is accessed by check.
16. Any other fees or penalties such as an NSF payment penalty.

The Truth-In-Lending Disclosure

The Truth-In-Lending disclosure (TIL) is required to be given to you by Regulation Z, a Federal law. This regulation protects you by providing you with your true cost of credit. This may or may not be a separate form. Many lenders include this disclosure with the note. If not, you will sign this form and receive a copy.

Some of the key items that are contained in a Regulation Z disclosure are as follows:

1. The identity of the lender and the borrower.
2. The finance-charge calculation method.
3. The APR and, if an open end loan, the periodic rate.
4. Whether or not there is a period where no finance charges will be assessed if the balance is paid in full on an open end loan.
5. How the balance is calculated on an open end loan, such as the average daily-balance method.
6. The minimum finance charge in any monthly billing period or cycle on an open end loan.
7. Any other charges associated with the loan.
8. Explanation of the conditions under which the lender can retain the security.
9. For open end loans, a statement of billing rights as directed by the Fair Credit Billing Act.
10. If you elect to take credit insurance with the loan, a section will indicate that credit insurance is included. If you do not elect to take credit insurance, then this section may just state that decision, and you would either initial or sign that box.

The Mortgage

The purpose of the mortgage is to collateralize your equity loan with real estate. This form is recorded where other real estate securities are recorded to show that a lien has been placed on your property and to validate that lien in the favor of the lender. You sign this document and retain a copy.

Normally, you will find the following items within the mortgage form:

1. Identification of both the lender and the borrower.
2. A detailed legal description of the property.
3. The amount of indebtedness for a closed end loan or the amount of the credit line if an open end loan.
4. The fact that you must pay when payments are due.
5. The fact that you must maintain the insurance and the taxes on the property even if these are to a different first mortgage lender.
6. Your responsibility to pay and fully maintain prior mortgage payments.
7. A requirement that the property must be kept in good condition and can be inspected by the lender with proper notice.
8. The lender's definition of events of default and the recourse available in the event of default. This is a very important clause because it says what must happen (*events of default*) before the lender can take action against you (*recourse*) and what the lender can do to you in those cases. These events of default are not necessarily limited to your stopping your payments. There are other things that might happen which would allow the lender to foreclose. It is essential that you understand what those events of default are and also that you understand what the actions of recourse are.

The Billing-Rights Statement

If you have an open end line of credit, then you are entitled to a billing-rights statement informing you of your billing rights under the Fair Credit Billing Act. You have the same billing rights for an equity line of credit as you do for your credit card. These rights include a number of things that you're allowed to do that are covered in Chapter Six in detail. Many times, this is contained in the agreement or handed to you as an informational brochure. In the brochure format, it need not be signed.

Other Riders

No, these are not cowboys. They refer to other documents that are part of a principal document,such as the mortgage or the agreement. They are as follows:

1. A two-to-four-family rider: Used if your property is multi-family and not single-family. If you are renting your second floor, for example, the lender may ask you to sign a separate document to that effect stating that if you fail to make payments, the lender has the right to collect the rents for you and apply those rentals to your monthly payment amounts.
2. A condominium rider: Used if the equity loan is for a condominium. Condominiums have special legal descriptions and owners' association rights that must be addressed from a legal standpoint.

Important Forms You'll See *after* the Closing

Although the dreaded closing is now over, there are still a few more documents with which you must deal.

Confirmation of Right of Rescission

This is a form you sign after the three-day waiting period has expired confirming that you do not want to cancel the loan.

There is an obscure section of the law that states that, in an emergency, you as a borrower have the right to waive the three-day right of rescission by stating in your own handwriting directly on the rescission form that this is an emergency. You can say something like: "I, as borrower, do hereby voluntarily waive my right of rescission because of the emergency nature of this loan." Most lenders, however, are very sticky on this point, and they will not let you exercise this waiving of the right of rescission unless it really is an emergency. So you can't use this law to get around the rescission period for the sake of convenience. Again, each obligated borrower who signed the original right of rescission must also sign this form and then receive a copy of it.

Billing Statement

Another document that is very important to your loan is called the billing statement. This is a document you will receive periodically as long as you have your home equity line of credit. This document, however, deals more with the servicing aspect of a line of credit and is covered in Chapter Six.

Costs You Can Expect at Closing

At closing you're going to have to cover a variety of different costs. Included among these costs are the following:

1. Points or the loan origination fee, also sometimes called the service charge. Usually this fee is expressed as a percentage of the total amount borrowed or the amount of the line of credit. For example, on a $20,000 line of credit, one percent or a one point orginination fee would be $200.
2. Appraisal fee. The appraisal fee is normally paid at closing. Appraisals can range from $75 to $225 depending on the amount of the loan requested and the type of appraisal done.
3. Credit-report fee. Credit-report fees are not charged by all lenders, but if your lender passes on these costs to you, you can normally expect to pay between $10 and $50 for the credit-report work. If your lender charged you an application fee, this most likely was included, and you need not pay it a second time.
4. Lender's inspection fee. If a lender makes an inspection of your house rather than having an appraisal done, you may have to pay a fee for this. Especially if the purpose of the loan is home improvement, the lender will need to inspect the home improvement prior to disbursing the final funds.
5. Insurance and taxes. Taxes are normally paid as part of the first mortgage. You can expect at least a statement within the documents you sign that it's your responsibility to maintain taxes. Hazard insurance, on the other hand, is required to be in place with the second mortgage lender as loss payee for at least

the amount of its loan. Insurance is something that needs to be taken care of prior to the closing, and there may be an additional charge from your real estate agent to add a separate loss payee.

6. Title charges. At closing you will be assessed for any title charges such as title examination, an abstract or title search, or perhaps the full title insurance binder. All these title items can basically be summed up as an ownership check of your real estate collateral to be sure you have ownership rights to it and that the only other claim would be the first mortgage.
7. Document preparation. Some lenders charge for the document preparation, but this is usually a small fee.
8. Attorney's fee. Depending on how the closing works, you may be charged for attorney's fees to do the closing.
9. Recording fees. Because the mortgage must be recorded, you will normally be charged recording fees. Usually these fees are minor and average less than $25.
10. Additional charges. Some additional charges could include a land survey or a pest inspection or some other inspection of the property, but these are usually rare on second mortgages.

Schedule

As we've stated, closings can be very confusing. All the forms have now been explained, and it may be worthwhile to go step-by-step through the scheduled procedure, so that you are not only familiar with the forms but also with the schedule.

When you apply for the loan, you sign and fill out the *application.* This is the last form you fill out until your loan is approved. While at the lender's institution, you will normally receive a *good-faith estimate* of how your loan would work, assuming you're approved.

If your loan is turned down, you will receive an *adverse-action form* through the mail. If your loan is approved, you will receive a *commitment letter* through the mail.

At the closing, you sign the *right of rescission*, the *note*, the *agreement*, the *truth-in-lending disclosure,* if that is a separate form, the *mortgage*, and the *billing-rights statement,* if this is a line of credit.

Three days after the closing, you sign the *confirmation of the right of rescission*. You then receive your money, either through your line being activated, a check being mailed to you or available for pickup at the lender's institution, or your account being credited for the amount of the loan.

And that's all there is to it!

Strategies

As you can see, a number of charges can occur at closing time. We recommend that you contact your lender prior to closing as to how they are handled. You will want to know if you have to pay these closing costs out of your own pocket at the time of closing or whether you can pay them with the proceeds of the loan. You also want a detailed breakdown of all charges prior to going to the closing, so you can anticipate what the costs may be. Also, if you have an objection about any of the closing costs or if you have a question about them, you will know ahead of time and will be prepared to question them at the closing.

As easy as we hope that we have made this sound, it will still probably take you longer to close your loan than it took you to read this chapter. But by knowing the documents that you will be signing at closing, you can be sure that nothing will come back to haunt you later.

Chapter Twelve

What to Do if You Get in Trouble

Now you finally have your equity line of credit or your home equity loan. The closing went smoothly, and you have your money. It is hoped that for the next five, ten, or 15 years you'll be making payments every month like clockwork. Nothing will ever happen that will cause you to be late with a payment or miss a payment or get in trouble with your lender. Right? Well, while this sounds good, it's not very realistic, especially for a longer term loan like 15 years.

In that 15-year period of time, you've got 180 months, 780 weeks, and 5,475 days. It is entirely possible, even probable, that at some point you could get in some trouble with this loan, even if it's just a late payment.

Is this unusual? Not really, although lenders like to think that responsible borrowers have some savings set aside for a rainy day. The rule of thumb is two or three months of take-home pay in a savings account to handle minor emergencies. But this isn't necessarily realistic in today's high-consumption environment.

Some of the things that can happen are relatively minor and can usually be accommodated by your lender. Other problems, however, which are more major may require some serious action. There are things you can do to prevent a minor problem from turning into a major one, and they usually involve working with your lender.

What do lenders do when payments aren't made? It would probably make your life easier, or at least you would sleep better, if you knew what sorts of actions were open to them. And what about the ultimate threat—foreclosure? This is the final collection technique—one you want to prevent at all costs.

This entire area can be divided into two sections—events of default and lenders' remedies. Events of default are those things that you do that threaten your paying back the loan. Lenders' remedies are those things that the lender does to assure that you do pay back the loan. Events of default can be minor, such as a late or missed payment, or major, such as filing bankruptcy. And lenders' remedies can be minor, such as sending you a late charge notice, or major, such as foreclosing on your house.

Minor Payment Delays

What are some of the minor difficulties you might get into? The most minor, and the one that is most likely to happen to you, is to have something cause you to submit a payment a few days or a week late. Another problem that might happen that is also relatively minor is to have one of your payment checks bounce. Here's what you can do in either of those cases.

Late Payment

Most lending agreements specify a due date for your payment, and if this due date is not met, then the lender may assess a late charge. A late charge is a penalty charged to your account for not making a payment on time. This charge can either be a flat amount, such as $5 or $10, or a percentage of either the outstanding balance or your monthly payment amount. Late charges are usually regulated by your state, so there could be as many as 50 different types of late charges throughout the United States today. Another factor that may figure into the late charge is whether your loan is considered a consumer loan or a real estate loan. Sometimes the lender is allowed to make this distinction, and sometimes state regulations decide. If your loan is considered to be a consumer loan, you generally pay a lower late charge. The late charge is always disclosed in your documentation, so it is easy enough to find out what the late-charge amount is. You can ask this question at closing or look in your documents.

Lenders will assess a late charge for two reasons. First, they want to discourage late payments. But secondly, a late payment really does require special handling. Additional costs are incurred, and a late charge helps cover those costs.

You should realize that two dates will be specified in your agreement—the loan-payment due date and the late-charge assessment date. It's easy to confuse these two dates. For example, your payment may be due on the first of every month. However, a late charge may not be assessed until the payment is more than 15 days late. Therefore, as long as a payment is made before the 16th of the month, you will not be assessed a late charge. You essentially have a 15-day grace period.

Many borrowers take advantage of this and play the float on the lender. They wait until the last possible moment before the late charge is assessed to make the payment. The danger in this tactic, however, is that if you make the payment on the 12th or 13th knowing that a late charge will be assessed on the 16th, any delay at all, including a delay in mail delivery, can wind up costing you some money. You can bear in mind, however, that lenders like to keep customers happy. Therefore, if you don't abuse the late-charge grace period and don't have more than one or perhaps two late payments per year, then it's quite likely that your lender will be willing to waive the late charge for you. This is something that you'd have to request, normally by phone, and at the same time promise not to be late in the future. Technically, if you are assessed a late charge and you made the payment any time other than on the first when it was due, you deserve the late charge. Your due date is the first, and if you wait until the 12th to pay, you are technically 12 days late.

Dishonored Payment

Another minor problem is if you make a payment on your equity loan and then your payment check bounces or doesn't clear. This can happen for a variety of innocent reasons. Perhaps a third-party check you deposited wasn't any good, or perhaps you didn't reconcile your checking account properly. If, of course, you were playing the float and your deposit didn't make it to the bank in time to cover the payment check, you deserved to have your check bounce!

At any rate, a payment may come back NSF (not sufficient funds), as an overdraft, or for some other return reason such as uncollected funds. You could have a dual problem. First, the lender to whom you made the payment could charge you a returned check charge. Second, the financial institution where you have your checking account on which you wrote the check could also charge you a fee. Together, these charges could add up to a significant amount, so you want to be careful that this doesn't happen. If you have both the loan and the checking account at the same institution, it's possible that this institution could then collect a double fee. Again, lenders like to keep their customers happy, so if you call the lender and straighten the matter out immediately, it's possible that they will waive the fee provided this doesn't happen too often.

Major Payment Delays

What happens if a more serious problem develops where payments are not only late but in danger of not being made at all? Usually the circumstances behind such a problem come from one of two causes. Either your income is suddenly reduced, or the amounts you have to pay have increased above what you originally had calculated when you borrowed the money. Either of these situations places a strain on your ability to repay the loan.

You need to do everything you possibly can to make a home equity payment. This is not just a credit card, where the lender may take you to court to get the money back, or an auto loan, where the lender may repossess the car. Here, the ultimate disaster may happen; the lender may throw you out of your house. So do everything you can to make this payment.

In the case where your income has been reduced, the first thing to ask yourself is, "What kind of income do I still have coming in?" Look at this very closely and compare your available income (inflow) with the bills and other obligations you have on a regular basis (outflow).

If the outflow has increased, then it's a matter of determining why. Then you have to make the really hard decisions and take a close look at your spending habits. The key here is to control your spending as much as possible before it gets out of hand.

Many times a payment on a debt is affordable even when you thought it wasn't. If you analyze your income and see what you can anticipate and then analyze your expenditures and see what is really necessary, you may find that you really can make this payment.

What happens if you really cannot make one or several payments due to a variety of circumstances? You may have been laid off from work, you're temporarily unable to work because of a disability or illness, or a relative may be seriously ill requiring high medical expenses. At any rate, whatever has happened can't be solved by simply cutting back expenses or dipping into savings. This leads you to the next step—working with your lender.

If you know that you're not going to be able to make the next month's payment and you also know that it's going to be awhile before you can make it, don't wait for your lender to contact you. *That's absolutely the worst thing you can do.* You must contact your lender and explain to the lender what the circumstances are. Lenders normally will work with you, especially when you contact them first.

When you do contact them, keep two things in mind that motivate lenders. First, they really do want that monthly payment and if they can't have it, they want to know why. Second, they don't want to be realtors. They don't want to repossess your house and then have to sell it.

Who should you contact with your problem? You can first try the loan officer that granted you the loan. Many times this person is not actively involved on the collection side but would be quite happy to try to help out people that he or she knows or has made loans to in the past. If this person can't help you or for some reason isn't appropriate, the next person you could contact is someone in the collections department. It is certainly preferable that you talk directly to the manager. That way you can cut through the red tape and start the process from the top. If you're dealing with a smaller institution, there's nothing wrong with going to the president. After all, this is your house and there is a lot at stake, so you want some heavy guns behind you when you explain what the problem is and request their help in working it out. Nothing makes the collections department more helpful than having you referred to them by the president.

But most important, and regardless of to whom you talk, you must contact the lender first. If you wait until the lender calls to ask where your payment is, it's too late. A bad impression is already created, and you'll have to work to erase that.

When you talk to the lender be very honest about when you think you can start making payments again and how much you can pay. Also, try to formulate some plan for catching up with any back payment amounts. The worst thing you can do is to make promises about payments knowing full well that they can't be kept. This will shortly wear out the patience of the lending institution and result in their saying, "Pay us now or we want the house."

What Lenders Do when Payments Aren't Made

Perhaps the best way to understand how lenders think of missed payments is to look at the process of collecting a past due account on a step-by-step basis. Collection departments of lending institutions work pretty much the same, as explained below.

Let's assume your loan is due on the first of the month. If the payment is not received by the first, the lender isn't very concerned. In fact, they don't even know the payment hasn't arrived yet.

Ten Days Late

By the tenth of the month, ten days have gone by and no payment has been received. At this point, some lending institutions have a computer program generate a notice that is mailed automatically. This notice is simply a gentle reminder that the payment has not been received and it's already ten days past due. Usually, it will also state that if payment has already been made, please disregard this notice. Many lenders have decided to eliminate sending out this reminder notice because they've found it has little effect on repayment habits. In fact, it may have a negative effect in that many borrowers think that they don't have to pay until they receive the reminder notice. The reminder notice is the trigger that makes them finally mail in the payment.

15 Days Late

Now let's assume you have 15 days before a late charge is assessed. So after 15 days no payment has been received, and on the night of the 15th after all the payments have been processed (therefore really the 16th day), a late charge is assessed. Now another computer-generated notice is mailed out. This notice states that the payment has not been received and that a late charge has been assessed for whatever the amount may be. You would know from the agreement not only the normal monthly payment but also the late charge amount. So assume your payment is $300 per month and the late charge is $5; you now owe the lender $305 .

What happens if you mail in a $300 check in two days? The $300 is supposed to be applied to your loan, but there is still a $5 late charge outstanding. The prevailing practice in the past was for lenders to first collect the late charge, which in this example is $5, and then only apply $295 to the loan. This then still leaves the borrower $5 delinquent, and another late charge is assessed next month. So you are being charged late charges on late charges, which is called *capitalization of late charges.* This is no longer legal in most states, and if this happens to you, you should challenge your lender over this practice. Now, in most states, the $300 you sent in must all be applied to the loan and the late charge is collected last.

Well, 16 days have gone by, no payments have been received, a late charge has been assessed on your account, and a late-charge notice has probably been sent to you in the mail. Usually, most lenders will allow another ten days for a response to the late charge notice. So you will not receive any additional notices or phone calls from your lender until 25 days have gone by. When you're 25 days late, the lender starts to get a little worried, because in another five days a second payment will be due.

25 Days Late

On the 25th day a lender has two options—either another letter can be sent or a phone call can be made. The more aggressive lenders will make a phone call at this stage or perhaps even earlier because they want to find out what the problem is. Less aggressive lenders will send another letter. A letter usually isn't very effective, because you certainly know your payment is past due and you have already received written communication from them in the form of a late-charge notice. If you had intended to respond to written communication, you would have already done so.

In any case, at the 25-day point another collection action will normally occur, and it will usually be a phone call. The lender will first try to call you at home with the second choice being at work. What the lender wants to know is why payment hasn't been made and why you haven't responded to the notices. Then the lender will work with you to determine some way to make payment on the loan. Any arrangement made is kept on either a computerized system or some sort of follow-up card or report, so that if you promise to make a payment by a certain date, then you can be sure that the lender will follow up on that date to see that it has arrived. If it hasn't arrived, you can anticipate another call.

Again it's important that you don't make promises that you don't expect to keep. If you promise something and it becomes apparent that you can't fulfill your promise, then it's your responsibility to contact the lender, tell them what happened, and then work out some new arrangement.

More than 25 Days Late

Let's assume the worst. You have a serious problem. You don't have the money to make the payment the first month, and you may not even have the money to make the payment the second month. So what do you do? You should have some idea about when you may have the money or what steps you can take to earn some income. If you're temporarily out of work on a layoff, then the lender could be comforted by the fact that you're scheduled to return within a certain period of time. If you can verify that through a letter from the personnel office where you work, then the lender will often delay on any further action. Or if you're trying to get another job and can verify that, perhaps with a schedule of job interviews, the lender may relax somewhat. The lender is primarily looking for any honest effort on your part that will eventually cure the default.

It is important that you realize that default isn't necessarily restricted to when you're late in payments; you may be in default of your contractual obligations with the lender.

Events of Default

The first event of default, when you're late with your payments, and what the lender can do, has already been covered above. But there are other events of default which a borrower might commonly run into.

These are listed below. If they apply to you, they will be stipulated in your loan agreement.

Failure to Pay Taxes

The lender will require that you pay your real estate taxes, and if you become delinquent on your taxes, then you will also be in default on the loan. If you fail to pay taxes, the lender can take actions against you, including foreclosure. You must maintain a current status on your real estate taxes, because if you don't the lender could lose the security interest in your property should your househave to be sold for taxes. In this case, the sale proceeds would first go to the government, and the lender would only get what is left over.

Failure to Pay Hazard Insurance

If you fail to pay your hazard insurance, this is also a condition of default. If some disaster happens to your house, then the lender could wind up with an unsecured loan because there's no insurance to cover the loss. It is quite possible for a lender to file foreclosure just because you failed to pay your insurance.

Waste of Property

The lender has the right to be sure that the property maintains its value because they loaned you money based on a certain value of the property. If the value of the property decreases because of negligence on your part, then the lender has the right to place your loan in default and seek all remedies that are available, which would be the same ones that could be used if you failed to make payments.

Death of Borrower

If the borrower dies, that could also be considered to be a default. In other words, because you died, you broke the contract with your lender. In reality, the lender's position in this case would be that they have rights within any estate in that they have a lien on the real estate. If the real estate goes into probate, then the lender maintains rights against that real estate for the balance of the loan.

Bankruptcy

The filing of bankruptcy is considered a default on the loan even if your loan is not delinquent. There are cases where individuals file bankruptcy but are not delinquent on their first or second mortgage loan. This doesn't matter, however, for many lenders, and they can go ahead and consider your loan in default. Bankruptcy will be covered in detail later, but basically even if your loan is considered in default, bankruptcy protects the debtor, so there is not a whole lot a lender can do against you.

False Information

If you've given any false information in filling out the application or given any false facts in the decision-making process when the lender granted the loan, this may also be considered an event of default.

Your Credit Changes

Adverse changes in your credit rating could affect an equity line of credit but not a closed end loan. To determine for yourself whether any credit changes would be considered adverse, ask yourself whether you think this lender would be willing to lend you the money they lent you before, based on your current financial condition and credit standing?

For an equity loan, you already have the money, and unless you stop making payments your lender can't do much to you if your credit slips. It would be foolish for them to call the entire loan due, which they may technically be allowed to do, because that would only guarantee that they wouldn't get their money. But for an equity line of credit, your lender may disallow any additional draws against your line because your credit has changed. If the lender feels that had you applied today you would have been disapproved, then with this clause in your agreement they have the right to restrict further draws. Lenders will normally check your credit annually or every 18 months.

Lenders' Remedies

Now, how long do you suppose the lender will hang on? Well, that answer can vary, but many times the lender is willing to wait as long as six months provided that there is some hope that things will get better. This doesn't mean that they will accept hollow promises where you have no intention of keeping your word or being able to follow through. Lenders with any degree of skill, especially in the collections area, can see through these tactics in a fairly short time. So if they detect that you're not going to make payments, there are various actions they can take beyond just working with you to collect the payments. These actions or *remedies* are generally spelled out in your agreement.

If you default or decide not to make payments on your loan, lenders have a number of remedies that they can pursue in order to get their money. Even if your situation is serious, you must still keep the perspective that the money you borrowed doesn't belong to you. The lender gave it to you in good faith that they would get it back. And the money doesn't even belong to the lender; it belongs to the savers at that institution. The lender has a responsibility to safeguard those funds for the people who put deposits in their institution.

If you want to know what actions the lender can take to get their money back, you can look in your home equity loan agreement. This will usually spell out the rights of the lender in case of default as well as the events of default. Now should any of these conditions of default listed above occur, then the lender could do a number of things.

Calling the Loan

First, the lender could call the entire loan due. When a lender does this, they send you a formal letter, usually registered with another copy sent through regular mail, stating that your loan is being called and that the entire balance is due and payable immediately. In reality, this tends to be a somewhat unrealistic move. If you're already past due and can't make two payments, then it's pretty unlikely that you can pay off the entire balance in one lump sum. However, one of the reasons lenders take this action is that it does meet a legal requirement of what's called *accelerating* or *calling* the loan.

If you pay off the full balance, maybe with money from a family member or from another lender, then the lender will take no further action. Why should they; they've gotten their money. But if you can't pay, then the lender can move on to more serious steps.

Right of Offset

The lender could invoke the right of offset, which is the right to take the money in any other account that you have with their institution, such as a checking or a savings account, and apply that toward your loan. They can't do this, however, with a fiduciary account such as an IRA or any account held in trust for a minor. If you know you're going to default on the loan and there's no reason to leave your savings account where it is, then you better not leave it with the same lender that has your loan. Otherwise, when your loan goes delinquent, the lender will take the money out of your account whether you want that or not.

Now, if you don't have the funds to make the payment and you don't have any funds that can be used to offset the payment, then the ultimate action a lender can take is to admit that they can't collect the loan from you and, therefore, they will have to collect it from the collateral. And the only way to collect the money from the collateral is to foreclose on your property.

Foreclosure: An Eleven-Letter Four-Letter Word

Foreclosure is the ultimate threat. How often does foreclosure happen? Well, if it's your house that's being foreclosed on, the answer is "too often!"

To foreclose on a property is a little like repossessing a car. The lender just takes the collateral back. But with real estate, it's not quite so easy. States have many protective laws to take care of consumers because of the time-honored tradition of respecting a man's (or woman's) home. So it's difficult for unscrupulous lenders to resort to this tactic. And that is as it should be.

While the process can vary dramatically from state to state, it can take anywhere from two months to 18 months or even longer. The first step is usually to consider the loan in default and accelerate or call the loan. When the borrower doesn't pay, the lender then files a foreclosure suit.

A foreclosure on a second mortgage differs somewhat from a foreclosure on a first mortgage, since the lender of the second mortgage is not the only one who has a lien on the property. They get paid only *after* the holder of the first mortgage gets paid the full amount outstanding on the first mortgage. So if you borrowed $20,000 on the second mortgage and you had $50,000 on the first mortgage, then the total indebtedness you would have against your property would be $70,000. The second mortgage lender, when they sold your house, would have to pay $50,000 to the first mortgage lender. This is a lot of money for the second mortgage holder and is one of the reasons why foreclosure doesn't happen very often.

Researching Other Liens

Because of this problem, the next step is to find out who else has rights in the property. This is done by researching the property to see if any other liens are registered against it, such as a first mortgage, a federal tax lien, a third mortgage, or any other type of interest. The second mortgage holder must then notify all interested parties, including you, of course, that foreclosure is being filed.

Going to Court

Foreclosure is a legal suit asking for judgment to be entered against you, the borrower, for you to pay the debt by surrendering the collateral to the second mortgage holder. This action is published in the paper and thus also serves notice to all other interested parties about whom the second mortgage holder may not know.

It could be a while before the suit goes to court, depending upon how heavy the court schedule is. When it does get to court, make sure you've hired a competent attorney to represent your side of the story. It's definitely not recommended that you act as your own attorney. This is one of those times when you want good legal counsel at your side. Once it goes to court, judges will usually side with the consumer against the bank. If you are prepared to offer any defense at all, the judge will usually postpone the court date to allow you to put your defense together. We've seen a number of cases where the judge took it upon himself to offer counsel to the debtor and order the lender to follow a plan to help the debtor. Reasonable plans usually include any in which you'd be making the normal monthly payments plus advancing some additional funds toward the back payments, usually in the range of one and one-half payments per month until the loan is brought up to date. You can't, however, always count on the judge doing this for you, so be prepared to offer a reasonable plan for repayment.

When all postponements are done and the case is tried, the lender will ask that judgment be entered for foreclosure.

Sheriff's Sale

Even when foreclosure is granted, it doesn't mean that you have to move out. Normally, the next step is that the lender forces the sale of the property. And this is not a normal sale but rather something called a *sheriff's sale*, which is a bidding process where the sheriff offers your property to the highest bidder. A number of different types of people bid on properties at sheriff's sales or auctions. If it appears that there will be some equity left in the property above the lenders' liens, there are people who make a living at going to sheriff's sales and buying properties at bargain prices. They then fix them up and sell them at a tidy profit. There are also people who regularly read the foreclosure notices in the papers and contact people who are being foreclosed upon and offer to buy their residence at a greatly reduced price. These are people who are again looking for a quick sale at below market price, so that they can make a tidy profit when they resell the property. Selling to one of these individuals is not one of our recommended alternatives. Slamming the door in their face is one of our recommended alternatives.

You are notified of the date for the sheriff's sale when it has been set. Keep in mind that you as a borrower at this point still have first priority in repaying the loan. But now, however, the lender will probably no longer be willing to accept just the payments that will bring the loan up-to-date; they'll want the full loan balance. So coming in with $900 won't help at all; you would need the full $20,000.

Redemption Period

Once the sheriff's sale is held, you technically no longer own the property. However, in some states there is what is called a redemption period. This is a certain period of days or even months where you have the right to attempt to redeem the property from the high bidder. The high bidder may have been your lender or some other third party. Your lender, the second mortgage lender, will usually bid an amount that will cover the first mortgage balance plus the second mortgage balance plus all court costs and foreclosure expenses. They're not looking to make a profit, so that is usually as high as they will bid. If there is substantial equity above that amount, then it is possible that a third party bidder will be the highest bidder and thus the successful one. If that is the case, the third party bidder must come up with the cash within a short number of hours. Then the second mortgage holder as well as the first mortgage holder will be paid off. Until the redemption period is up, you still have a right to be within the property.

Vacating the Property

Now what happens if the redemption period expires and you are still living in the house? Well, you are now living in someone else's house, because, as the redemption period expires, the title passes to the successful bidder. You still have some options even at this stage. If your lender purchased the property, then they will want to sell it. If sales are slow, they may allow you to stay in the residence until they can sell the property. It's always better to have someone in the residence than to have it vacant ,because too many things can happen to a vacant house. And lenders know that the property will be of more value to them as long as it's lived in. The main concern the lender will have is whether you will leave on your own when the time comes. If you can convince the lender that you will stay there only until the property is sold, it is quite likely you will be allowed to stay. In fact, in many cases you can pay reduced rent or sometimes no rent at all. It is quite acceptable for you to negotiate with your lender to let you stay in the property until such time as it's sold if you agree to willingly leave once the property is sold.

Your ultimate option is just to refuse to leave at all. Then the lender must go through eviction proceedings, which again could take a couple of months. And during that period of time your lender is concerned that you could do some damage to the property. It's also very dificult for them to either market or sell the property while eviction proceedings are underway. They would much rather have you leave on your own after living in your house at reduced rent for a period of time. You would, however, have to maintain the property, such as cutting the grass, so that the property looks presentable to any potential buyer. If you don't agree to do this, then the lender would order you out because you would be threatening a potential sale.

Alternatives to Foreclosure

What are your options if foreclosure happens to you? There are always options, although at this stage of the game, they're not very attractive.

Refinancing

First, you could ask the lender for additional funds. That's pretty farfetched, though, because lenders are hesitant to lend you more money if you can't afford to pay the first loan. This situation only happens if you're Brazil or Mexico! However, if you get called back to work after a layoff, and you can convince the lender that you're back to work for the foreseeable future, they may be willing to renegotiate or refinance your loan. Whether or not you get additional funds, or new money as it is called, is up to the lender, but that probably happens less than half the time.

Normally, what will be done is to take all the missed payments and add them to the loan, refinance the loan, and in essence extend the term. For example, if you've missed payments for four months because you were laid off but are now back to work, the lender may allow you to pick up your payments where you left off, and the term of your loan would be extended four additional months. That's a short term solution and one that can be used if you can prove that your reduction in income has only been temporary.

Selling Your Residence

If you feel that the lender is going to foreclose and you see no other alternative, there is always a possibility that you could sell your residence on yourself to get the cash to pay off the lender. In addition, while you could attempt to sell it on your own without outside help, usually time is of the essence, and you can accelerate the process by using a realtor. So in all probability you'll have to pay some realtors' commissions.

But this is certainly worth a try before the lender comes in and takes your home away. Remember, if the lender winds up with your property and sells it for something higher than the balance on your loan, usually lenders don't have to return that. Any profit made on the sale of foreclosed property remains with the lender and does not go back to the original borrower. While this is not true of personal goods, such as automobiles, it is true of real estate. So, you should always at least try a sale on your residence rather than going all the way through foreclosure. Not only might you wind up with a profit, but if you can sell before the foreclosure process is completed, then it is possible that you won't have as bad a credit record on your credit bureau report. At least you won't have a foreclosure listing on your report.

Deed-in-Lieu

Another option is called *deed-in-lieu.* This is short for deed in lieu of foreclosure. Here you would go to the lender and say, "I'll tell you what. Here are the keys to my house. You don't foreclose against me and put a foreclosure on my credit record, and I will give you my house without a fight." Normally, you would only do this if sale were not a possibility and you had no equity in the property.

Lenders like this option because it costs them a lot less. An average foreclosure will cost at least $1,200, but if you give them the property, they have the opportunity to market it right away. They haven't spent $1,200 in legal fees and the house hasn't gone through the wear and tear of a foreclosure. In fact, in some cases lenders are willing to offer token amounts, $100 to $500, to individuals willing to sign over their deed because they are saving a considerable amount of money.

Deed-in-lieu would work as follows. Once you decide that you can't save the property, that you're going to lose it, and that you can't sell it yourself, you would contact the lender and offer them the option of accepting the property. The lender will normally say yes. But first they will want to check on any other liens. Remember that this second mortgage holder is obligated to pay off the first mortgage lender. But, in addition, if there is a third mortgage, the second mortgage lender is also obligated to pay them off. In a foreclosure court action, the second mortgage lender only has to pay off the first; any liens that come after the second would be left without anything unless they also join the legal action. So if there are other liens, the lender would probably not take a deed-in-lieu and would instead let the action go to foreclosure.

Bankruptcy

An additional alternative is to file bankruptcy which delays but does not stop a foreclosure suit. Bankruptcy is the ultimate option of a consumer. What bankruptcy does is to reschedule your debts, so you may, for example, have smaller payments over a longer period of time. Most important, you will now be repaying your debts under court supervision, meaning your debtors cannot take any action against you, including hassling you, sending collection agencies after you, or repossessing your property. It should only be used as a last resort and only if your debts are such that you cannot reasonably be expected to pay them back as they stand. Filing bankruptcy will stop any foreclosure action dead in its tracks. It will not, however, stop it forever. It merely postpones the inevitable if you really can't make payments on your mortgage loan.

If you plan on filing bankruptcy, then it's wise to consult a good bankruptcy attorney, specifically one who is familiar not only with real estate but also bankruptcy. The attorney can then provide you with insight as to what you can expect should you file bankruptcy at this point in time and depending on where your lender may be in the foreclosure process.

Just remember that filing bankruptcy will only postpone your debt. Bankruptcy does not erase a second mortgage. If you owe the money, you still have to pay it and if you can't, even though you filed bankruptcy, once the bankruptcy is completed, the foreclosure process will begin again.

Strategies

OK, so what do you do to survive in tough times? To summarize, try to follow these basic rules:

1. Always contact your lender immediately when you know there is going to be a problem. Remember, lenders don't want your house, they want their money back and they want to keep a customer. Their outlook is that if they can help you over this difficult period of time you will be a good and loyal customer for years to come.

2. Never play games with lenders. If you promise to deliver something, then deliver it. If you cannot make a payment, then be up front and state that you can't and advise them how long it will be before you can.

3. If your ability to repay has been reduced for a temporary period of time, approach your lender with the idea of refinancing the loan, in other words extending the term.

4. If you have an extended delay and are unable to make repayments and ultimately face loss of your property, then look at the alternatives of sale, deed-in-lieu, or perhaps even bankruptcy.

It's your house and it's your home. Taking care of it should be your top priority. Don't take delinquency lightly, because your lender does not. While anyone can experience tough times now and then, it's really up to you as to how well they are handled.

Appendix

Monthly Payment Calculator
Term of Equity Loan in Years

Rate	*5 Years*	*10 Years*	*15 Years*	*20 Years*
7.0	$19.80	$11.61	$8.99	$7.75
7.5	20.04	11.87	9.27	8.06
8.0	20.28	12.13	9.56	8.36
8.5	20.52	12.40	9.85	8.68
9.0	20.76	12.67	10.15	9.00
9.5	21.01	12.94	10.45	9.33
10.0	21.25	13.22	10.75	9.66
10.5	21.50	13.50	11.06	9.99
11.0	21.75	13.78	11.37	10.33
11.5	22.00	14.06	11.69	10.67
12.0	22.25	14.35	12.01	11.02
12.5	22.50	14.64	12.33	11.37
13.0	22.76	14.94	12.66	11.72
13.5	23.01	15.23	12.99	12.08
14.0	23.27	15.53	13.32	12.44
14.5	23.53	15.83	13.66	12.80
15.0	23.79	16.14	14.00	13.17
15.5	24.06	16.45	14.34	13.54
16.0	26.32	16.76	14.69	13.92

This chart shows what your monthly payment is for a loan of $1,000 at a given rate and term. For example, an 8 percent rate for 10 years results in a monthly payment of $12.13 per $1,000 borrowed. If you borrowed $25,000, then your payment is 25 x $12.13 or $303.25 per month.

Index